THE Joy OF Yarn

Your Stash Solution for Curating, Organizing and
Using Your Yarn—with 10 Knitting Patterns

Marie Greene

PAGE STREET
PUBLISHING CO.

PAGE STREET
PUBLISHING CO.

First published in 2023 by

Page Street Publishing Co.

27 Congress Street, Suite 1511

Salem, MA 01970

www.pagestreetpublishing.com

Distributed by Macmillan, sales in Canada by The Canadian Manda Group.

27   26   25   24   23   1   2   3   4   5

ISBN-13: 978-1-64567-926-4

ISBN-10: 1-64567-926-8

Library of Congress Control Number: 2022950261

Cover and book design by Rosie Stewart for Page Street Publishing Co.

Photography © 2023 Annie Loaiza

Illustrations by Carlee Wright

Printed and bound in China

Dedication

For my husband Scott, who has patiently hauled my
(ridiculously large) stash from one house to another
many times during our thirty years together and has
never once suggested I have too much yarn.

Contents

Introduction

I learned to knit before the Internet, before craft rooms were a thing and long before anyone talked about the joy of tidying. Staying organized was never part of my creative vocabulary. I just wanted to collect supplies and make things. It never occurred to me that one day I might have so much yarn—and so many needles—that I would need a system to keep them from taking over my home.

My knitting grandma, Margie, kept her yarn in plastic bags tucked in closets and corners, under beds, behind doors and even in her barn. An actual barn. *Where goats lived.* Sure, she taught me how to knit, but she also taught me to hold on to every scrap and tidbit of yarn like my life depended on it. Waste not, want not. If a little yarn is good, then a lot of yarn is better.

It was only when my own stash began spilling out into practically every room in the house that I realized there is a difference between stockpiling yarn just for the sake of having it and having the yarn I needed for what I wanted to make. The secret to an incredible stash (which I didn't know at the time) is having the right yarn—and being able to find it.

This book is for my fellow overwhelmed yarn stashers who love to buy, squish, store and use yarn. It's for those who want to do their part to keep their local yarn stores and yarn makers in business, but who also know that if they don't come up with a plan for their stash, they may have to use it to insulate the walls of their home. It's for everyone who's ever tried and failed a yarn diet (been there, done that, zero stars, do not recommend). This book is for those who feel disorganized and uninspired when they look at their yarn stash and who know there must be a better way. If you aren't already head over heels in love with your stash, I wrote this book for you. It doesn't matter where you are as you begin this journey, whether you're in a studio apartment or in a house with a dedicated yarn room. I've worked with fiber artists across the world and from every walk of life who have used these same tools to transform their stash. And you can, too.

If you could see what my stash looked like ten years ago, you would know that I did not come quickly to this place of getting organized. I spent years shopping and stashing with reckless abandon, often holding on to yarn that I didn't even really want. I was like the ill-fated hero in Samuel Taylor Coleridge's poem, except it wasn't water I was drowning in; it was wool. *Yarn, yarn everywhere. And not a skein to knit.*

If your stash is full of yarn, but none of it is the yarn you need for your project, I wrote this book for you.

There's a spot in the middle—between impulse shopping and yarn diets—where the magic of an intentional creative space happens. I went from testing these principles at home to teaching them to knitters around the world in my bestselling Stash Sprint workshops. I've watched in real time as knitters of all abilities, income levels and circumstances have tackled their stash monsters and lived to talk about it. I've seen my students make the transition from feeling completely overwhelmed about their yarn stash to being confident, relieved and inspired.

This process works.

My stash system can help you transform more than just your knitting supplies, but yarn is the best place to start because it's the one thing in our homes that other organizational books and methods don't completely acknowledge (at least not to the degree that we need them to). Yarn isn't just "stuff," and no one knows that better than we do. If we can create order amidst the chaos of the yarn in our homes, we can do anything.

This is not a book about yarn diets, and if it was, I would not be the one to write it because I very publicly failed at mine. Instead, this is a book about how to buy the yarn you'll use, how to find inspiration in the yarn you already have and how to let go when your heart tells you that some yarn is meant for a better life elsewhere. This is a book about the space you have and how you fill it. We'll talk about what drives your yarn choices and how to shop for the yarn you actually want (and need), instead of the yarn your friend said looks great with your eyes. (Sometimes the yarn you want and the yarn your friend wants for you are the same, but not always.)

If you've ever worried that your stash will outlive you or felt overwhelmed trying to get yourself organized, this book is for you. No guilt trips. No yarn diets. This is your chance to finally put things in order and curate a yarn collection you will LOVE . . . *and use.*

Marie Greene

Assessing Your Fiber Real Estate

Most of us are buying, storing and shifting around a lot of yarn we're never going to use. But we can't get rid of it because:

A. It's perfectly good yarn

B. It wasn't cheap

C. It holds sentimental value and/or

D. We might need it someday

It doesn't matter if you have a house full of perfectly good yarn if it's not the type of yarn you're looking for. Or if the yarn you're looking for is in there somewhere, but you can't find it, then what good is it? Having yarn just for the sake of having it isn't the stash strategy we'd like to think it is, and it's likely consuming more than its share of space in our homes.

Even yarn that looks organized can be deceiving. There's a difference between looking good and being useful. My stash has endured many face-lifts that faded because I was trying to make it look better without diagnosing the source of the problem. I knew my stash wasn't working for me, but I couldn't put the reason into words; it was simultaneously too much and not enough. How do you diagnose that? And how do you fix a problem you can't identify?

In this chapter, we'll redefine the meaning of "stash," calculate the space you're devoting to it (and what that space is costing you) and lay the foundation for the journey ahead.

Reinventing Your Stash

Is it any wonder that the word "stash" feels uninspiring when the word itself is synonymous with small quantities, oddballs, scraps and leftovers? It's like we're not even giving it a chance.

So, let's start by defining what stash yarn **really** is: It's just yarn that you already own. That's it.

What's IN your stash is an entirely different story. It might be a hodgepodge of leftovers, hand-me-downs and yarn that seemed like a good idea at the time, but your stash has the potential to be a beautifully curated collection that suits your knitting personality, fits your space and inspires your creativity. If you don't know what's in your stash, never seem to have the right yarn for the job or if it takes ages to find what you're looking for, there is hope. And there is a better way.

Like many bold knitters who have come before me, I've tried (and failed) my share of yarn diets. But my last yarn diet—the biggest failure of them all—was the one that finally made everything click. That period of attempted self-control did not result in me going a year without buying yarn, but it DID draw a line in the sand and change the way I thought about the yarn I was keeping at home.

Before the Yarn Diet (BYD), I owned colors, quantities and yarn weights that I would NEVER use (as evidenced by the fact that I'd held on to them for decades and they never once rose to the surface as a viable option for a project). Every time we moved to a new house, these *perfectly-good-but-not-great* yarns were packed up and hauled along with us. They took up space in my closets and became an invisible albatross. I stopped noticing they were even there, but that didn't keep them from getting in my way when it came time to dig around and find something . . . *anything* . . . that might work for my next project.

After the Yarn Diet (AYD), I began to think of my stash as my home yarn shop—a place to store the kinds of yarn I use most, instead of a graveyard for all the yarn I felt too guilty to give away. I started to recognize the limitations of my space, and I learned to love having a little bit less yarn in my house because I knew that what I DID have was the right stuff. With a limited amount of space, I had to make sure that I wasn't wasting any of it on yarn I'd never use. If you're a sock knitter who never knits sweaters, maybe having a bunch of sweater quantities isn't the best use of your yarn shelf. If you live in a warm climate and mostly knit lightweight summer tops, does it make sense to have a closet full of chunky weight yarn? Figuring out what you have and what you use makes it easier to decide what deserves space on your shelf.

It's time to change the definition of "stash" and start thinking of it not as a bunch of scrappy leftovers, but instead as your own personally curated yarn shop, so you can get to the good work of making it useful and inspiring. Roll up your sleeves, friend. Good things await.

Where Is Your Yarn Hiding?

Once upon a time, my yarn was compartmentalized into project bags, closets and shelves, but I never thought of it as a whole. What did my stash—as an entity—say about my personality as a maker? About my style as a knitter? I knew vaguely what I had—or at least I thought I did—but I didn't know exactly *how much* I had altogether, nor how much space it consumed in my home. Spreading it around the house in baskets and bags allowed me to believe that what I was storing was much more useful than it really was. After all, if it's in a project bag, then you're obviously using it for a project, right? I bet there's a skein of yarn (or five) in a project bag somewhere in your home that could disappear without a trace, and you wouldn't even notice.

Stash compartmentalizing is one of the most common ways we cope with a yarn collection that's gotten out of control, so before we start organizing, how about a quick reality check? Let's do the math to find out how much space your yarn is consuming, and what that space is costing you in actual dollars. You're about to see your yarn stash in a very different light.

You'll need:

- A tape measure (and possibly a friend to help you hold it)
- Paper
- A pen
- A calculator
- An open mind

Take a walk around your home, and peek inside your cupboards, drawers and closets—anywhere that yarn might be hiding. Don't take anything out or move it around (yet); this is strictly a fact-finding mission, and it's meant to be brief. You're not doing an appraisal, so estimates and approximates will do the job.

Measure the approximate size of the areas where you're storing yarn. If it's an entire basement, jot down the square footage of the basement. If it's a room, measure the length and width of the room and multiply those two numbers together to determine the square footage of that space. For example, a room that is 10 feet (3 m) long and 8 feet (2.5 m) wide has 80 square feet (7.5 square m) of space.

If you're storing yarn in multiple, smaller spaces—like closets and dressers—count how many of them you're using, and how many you have in total. For example, if you have four closets in your home and two of them are being used to store yarn, then you're currently giving up 50 percent of your closet storage to hold yarn. It might not seem like much in the scheme of things, but closets are high-value real estate. The fewer closets you have, the more valuable each one is.

Questions That'll Keep You Stuck

Q: Should I count the whole guest room if the yarn is only in the closet, under the bed and tucked into two armoires and one dresser in that room?

A: If a guest arrived at your doorstep unannounced, would you have to move yarn out of the way to make space for them? If the answer is yes, it's a yarn room and it counts.

Q: But I'm only using half of this closet to store yarn—can I just count half the closet?

A: If your closet is neatly organized and can store both yarn AND the household things you originally intended to store in there (broom? coats? vacuum?), then go ahead and count half a closet. But if you can't see the broom through the bags of yarn, then count the whole darn thing and keep going.

Q: My yarn is stored under beds, which is basically bonus space, right? Do I need to count that?

A: I hate to answer a question with another question, but how well is that "yarn under the bed" system working out for you? It doesn't matter how unimportant that space may seem; if you're using it to store yarn, it counts as yarn space. You don't have to count the whole room, but you could measure the length and width of the bed, multiply those together, and come up with the square footage to add to your calculation.

Do you see a pattern here?

If you're pausing to ask the question, "Does this count?" the answer is yes. It counts.

Calculate the square footage of all the yarn in your home (to the best of your ability) and add those numbers together. This is your current YSF (yarn square footage).

Your Yarn Square Footage

Now that you have a sense of how much space yarn is taking up in your home, you're ready for the next step. Take your monthly housing cost (rent or mortgage) and divide it by the total number of square feet in your home. For example, if you pay $2,000 USD a month to live in a home with 2,000 square feet, $2,000 divided by 2,000 square feet = $1.00 per square foot. (These may or may not be reasonable numbers where you are; this is merely an example.) If you want to be really accurate, you can factor in the cost of utilities and other monthly maintenance, but for the sake of brevity, let's say it's costing you $1.00 USD per square foot per month to live in your home.

Multiply your YSF times your monthly housing cost per square foot. Let's say your YSF is about 60 square feet in total. If you're spending $1.00 per square foot for your living space each month, it's costing you $60.00 per month to store yarn.

What is it costing you over the course of a full year?

> $60.00 x 12 = $720.00 USD per year for yarn storage. Over 5 years, you would have spent $3,600 USD for the use of that space.

Notice we're not talking about what it cost to buy the yarn (that's a conversation for another day, *or not at all, now that I think about it*); we're just talking about the value of the space you've devoted to the yarn you've been keeping—maybe for a very, very long time.

We're spending our hard-earned money—and giving up valuable space—to store yarn we may not even like, aren't using effectively and can't keep organized enough to find what's in there, anyway.

How much is it costing you to store your yarn collection? The numbers might be a bit startling at first, but it's powerful to see your stash as something more than just having some yarn around the house. Your stash may be taking up more space—and causing more frustration—than you realize. The good news is that there's something you can do about it.

> *"I got a little stuck on the real estate issue. I needed a whole ranch, but only had a small cottage available. But now that I'm actually pulling it out and sorting it, it's not that overwhelming."*
>
> —CYNTHIA A., STASH SPRINT STUDENT

If you find yourself wishing you had more space for your yarn, you're certainly not alone. But learning how to work with what you DO have is the key to falling in love with your stash. Now that you have the lay of the land, it's time to figure out what's *in* your yarn collection and how you'd like to organize it.

Organizing with the Three Cs: Content, Categories and Containers

The yarn you already own tends to become part of the background of your home. You see it, but you don't really *see* it, if you know what I mean. It's a lot like how you don't notice how messy your front room is until the doorbell rings. Clutter becomes invisible after a while, especially if you've squirreled it away in compartments like project bags, totes, shelves and drawers. Compartments exist to help you stay organized (in theory), but they make it difficult to see what you have—and that is both a blessing and a curse. You've probably been looking at the same drawers full of yarn for years, but as with just about everything else in your home, the more you get used to looking at something, the less you notice it. And the less you notice it, the more out of control it is likely to get.

In this section, we're going to get the lay of the land by bringing every skein of yarn out into the open. This is your chance to shed light on what you have so you can bring your entire stash into focus. And then you'll sort those skeins into categories that make sense for the way you keep and use yarn. After that, you'll figure out how you want to contain and store your fiber collection so that it fits your space and inspires you every time you see it. We'll turn chaos into order, and we'll do it one skein at a time.

What we won't do—at least not yet—is start putting things away. Putting things away without the right plan is one of the reasons we're here in the first place. It's how you end up with yarn bags on top of yarn bags inside of other yarn bags. There's a difference between getting something out of the way and putting it where it belongs. Having a very clear vision of where everything in your stash belongs and why it's there, which we'll get to in Step Four: Deciding What Stays (and What Goes) (page 49), will make it easy to get organized now and stay organized over time.

This chapter is a fundamental part of that process. It's how you figure out exactly what's in your creative space and where, specifically, everything should live. Until you know these two things, you can't put anything away. If you do, you'll be right back where you started in no time. I say this with personal authority as one who has done it that way more times than I can count, and who has finally learned to break my own cycle of disorganized chaos.

In the beginning, organizing your yarn is a lot like organizing the clothes in your closet—if you want to do it right, you can't just skim the hangers or rearrange things. You've got to take everything out so you can try things on and see what still fits. Let's apply that same mindset to your yarn stash by getting a handle on what you have (content), deciding on the right system for sorting it (categories) and assessing your space so you'll know how to maximize your resources (containers).

This chapter is about laying the foundation for a system that will keep you organized for the long term. Sure, it's tedious. And, at first glance, you might not think you need to do this part. (News flash: Yes, you do.) I've worked with thousands of knitters, and this part of the process is powerful. It's where the biggest AHA! moments are, and it will change your relationship with your yarn stash forever.

"After literally touching every single skein of yarn, making the decision to keep each one, and organizing it all, I no longer have a desire to buy every single colorway I see advertised . . . It's absolutely astounding. That's not to say that I won't get more yarn, but I am committed to the space I've designated, and it is FULL of beautiful stash that I explicitly decided to keep."

—KRIS J., STASH SPRINT STUDENT

I've watched people from every walk of life, even those with health limitations, busy schedules and overwhelming amounts of yarn, power through this process and come out the other side feeling liberated. It doesn't matter how much yarn you have, how much it cost you, how big or small your home is or what kind of budget you have for getting things into shape. I've seen it all and nothing could surprise me.

I'm your wing-woman, and we'll do this together.

Content: Getting Up Close and Personal with What's in Your Stash

Getting everything out in the open might be one of the more humbling moments in your yarn career. It's not always easy to look at your hobby from the eye of the storm, and chances are there will be moments when it will seem as if a tornado has ripped through your craft closet. But getting everything out in the open is the only way to find out what you're up against.

This is an excellent project for a long weekend, but there's no rule that says it must be finished in a few days. I've worked with knitters and crocheters who spent a month working through their stash, and others who managed it in a day or two. Depending on the size of your stash and how much time you have on your hands (not to mention your energy level), you may need a few days or a few weeks to get through it. That's okay. If you can devote a whole room to this project (at least temporarily), then you can close the door and walk away periodically until it's finished. But I'll warn you: The longer it drags on, the harder it gets. The sooner you can get through this hard part, the better you will feel.

Prepare Your Space

We're about to dump everything out. (And by we, I mean you, but I'll be with you in spirit.) But before you do, start with a clean space. It's important. Do a cursory cleanup of any surfaces that you'll use for sorting or holding yarn, even if it's only temporarily. Vacuum and sweep the entire space (including the corners) before you begin. This might sound like a tedious extra step, but carpet beetles and moths would just LOVE to get their chompers on your stash. Don't let them! If you're working on a tabletop, wipe it down and make sure it's clean and dry before you dump yarn all over it.

Spread out a large, clean, flat sheet or blanket over the surface or floor where you'll be sorting your yarn. This will make it easy to scoop everything up if you need to put it away quickly (in case you need the space for other things), and it will keep your skeins off the floor while you work. One of my personal stash rules is that I never let yarn sit directly on the floor because I don't want to accidentally transfer a new critter from the floor to my yarn shelves.

Gather a few large, clean boxes or trash bags so there's a place to put yarn barf (e.g., tangled bits of leftovers), old labels and obvious giveaway skeins when you find them. You might as well get them out of the way as soon as you see them.

Gather and Dump

Gather every ounce of yarn you've been hiding in your house and dump it out onto your prepared space. Haul the bins, the bags and the baskets. Leave no closet untouched, no project bag left behind. Seeing everything out in the open may tempt you to start sorting right away, but sit tight, as it's important to set eyes on what you have first.

Keep your WIPs (works in progress) together in one area, and leave them in their project bags for now. If they're not in bags, drop them into bags so you can keep them safe and separate from the rest of your stash. But instead of just piling them up, have a quick peek at these ongoing projects so that you can keep an eye out for matching skeins that may be elsewhere in your stash. There's nothing worse than thinking you've run out of yarn on a project, only to later realize there was one more skein hiding somewhere else.

When I say dump everything out, I really do mean it. Don't be shy about it. Empty the bins, drawers, shopping bags and whatever else you're using to hide yarn. If you're worried about judgment, or just don't want any witnesses to the chaos that's about to ensue, plan to do this at a time when you can really dive in and not worry about what anyone else thinks or says. This is your stash adventure, and the only opinion that really matters is yours.

Caution: You will face temptations as you sort your stash. You may even find the exact yarn you needed for the shawl you've been wanting to cast on. But hold that thought—if you can resist the urge to procrasti-knit right now, you'll get to the finish line faster.

As soon as you've gathered all your yarn together in one central spot, it's time to figure out how you're going to sort it.

Categories: Sorting by Color, Weight or Project

Every single time I reorganized my stash over the years, it required a complete overhaul. It was almost like I hadn't even TRIED to be organized, except that I **had** been trying—almost constantly—to maintain some semblance of order. But nothing I did seemed to last. *Maybe yarn just isn't meant to stay organized,* I thought. *Maybe creativity is inherently messy, and this is just as good as it gets?*

What was I missing? *Categories and containers.*

The Reasons I Thought My Yarn Was Disorganized

1. I buy too much yarn, a problem I am unwilling to solve, because new yarn makes me incredibly happy (and is usually cheaper than therapy). And I've already discovered that a yarn diet is not for me.

2. I need fancier shelves and more labels.

3. I need more containers.

4. My house is too small.

Nope, nope, nope and nope.

Fixing the Wrong Problems

After years of sincere attempts at getting organized, I had what I thought was an epiphany about how to get my yarn under control once and for all—and it was this misguided revelation that finally helped me realize that the source of my problem was not what I thought it was. In fact, I was making things harder than they needed to be by fixing the wrong problems.

My solution, if we want to call it that, was a more elaborate system of categories. I organized everything by both quantity AND weight, and piled it all into the most efficient, large containers I could find. In my mind, fewer containers = extra organized. Goodbye yarn clutter, hello super-organized craft closet! I'm so clever!

I very neatly filled two large, completely opaque plastic totes with oddballs and leftovers. I filled several more of these totes with single and double skeins, sorted by weight, and I also separated sweater quantities by weight. I stacked my newly arranged containers four totes high in a closet in my office and stacked the rest along one wall. I labeled every tote because that's just the kind of organizing genius I am. And then I waited for the magic of finally being organized to pay off.

That moment never came.

I found myself constantly unstacking totes and digging around trying to find what I was looking for. I would forget what I had, especially anything in or near the bottom layer of any given tote. I would have to sort through an entire bin (or four) to find one leftover bit of a very specific yarn to repair a hole in a sock. And if I had leftovers and full skeins of the same yarn, I would have to look in two different places to find them. My brilliant new system unraveled right before my eyes.

The Real Reasons My Yarn Was Disorganized

1. My yarn categories were too complicated.
2. My containers were too big.
3. I couldn't see my stash.
4. I was keeping a lot of yarn I was never going to use.

Why Categories Matter

Categories make it easy to establish meaning and order and, when it comes to creativity, that kind of structure can make it easier for inspiration to find you. History would have us equate creativity with chaos, but every crafter I know is far more delighted by art, beauty and order than by having to sift through a mountain of mess. Sorting yarn into simple categories eliminates the guesswork and makes it easier to put your stash to good use.

Having an organized, beautiful, and well-curated stash is a very different experience than digging through plastic bags piled on top of each other in a closet. There's a reason it's more fun to shop at your favorite yarn store than in your own stash, but you can re-create

some of that spark by borrowing a page from their playbook. After all, your stash is an extension of all your favorite places to shop, so it makes sense to create your own shoppable categories that make it easy for you to use what you bring home.

Color, Weight or Project: Choosing How to Sort

There are two tried and true methods that make it easy to stay organized: sorting by color or sorting by weight (but not both). There's a third option—sorting by project—which isn't as universally helpful but is right for certain people, so it's worth including. The category you choose will depend on what's in your stash, how you use it and where you're going to keep it.

Here are the pros and cons of each of these three methods, along with a few tips to help you decide which one might work best for you.

Category 1: Sorting by Color

Sorting by color may not be the first thing you think of when you're attempting to whip your stash into shape. It wasn't an immediate option in my mind, either. But hear me out.

When I first sorted my stash by color, it had nothing to do with being organized. In fact, for once in my yarn-loving life, I specifically didn't consider anything but aesthetics. I just wanted it to LOOK organized. Our youngest son had moved home (into the space formerly known as my office), so I moved my yarn to a small studio away from home. It was a bright, airy location, and it inspired me to spiff things up a bit. I stacked white cube shelves and sorted my yarn into a rainbow—purely for looks, mind you. I loved the way that wall of color welcomed me every time I walked through the door. It was like having my own little yarn shop.

Over the course of that year, I constantly dug through those shelves to find yarn for my projects. I quickly refilled them with my latest purchases (of which there were many). I scanned them for the right shade of gold or coral. I could see at a glance if I still had a skein of the gray I had used for my last sweater because I wanted to make a matching hat. It was . . . easy. In my attempt to make things pretty, I accidentally made them useful. In fact, my "let's pretend I'm organized" plan had become the single best organizational system I had ever used, and I did it on accident.

It's obvious when something isn't working because it's frustrating and gets messy fast. But when things are easy, you hardly think of them at all, and that's how you know you're onto something. I went from struggling with my stash to USING it, and I didn't even notice it was happening. I fell in love with my yarn again and had a lot more fun shopping for—and from—my stash. It was only when it was time to move my stash back home that I started thinking about whether or not I wanted to keep the rainbow cube system that had worked so well for me at my office. I mean, if it's just for looks and no one else sees it but me, does it really matter how cute it is?

But I realized that my pretend approach to being organized was more than just pretty on the surface. It was the perfect system for me, and it held up for an entire year with no extra effort. I never thought I'd be an advocate for a wall of rainbow-sorted yarn as the ideal way to organize your stash—it seems too simple, doesn't it? But it has worked better for me—and for many of my students—than anything else.

Advantages

- Arranging by color allows you to use your yarn as a decorative element in your space without looking cluttered.

- Seeing your color spectrum at a glance can make it easier to choose pairings for your next project.

- You will see right away when there are colors missing, making it easier to know what to shop for.

- You'll also notice when there's an odd skein that matches absolutely nothing in your stash and probably needs to be rehomed. (There was a certain murky olive-green skein that got the boot when I could visibly see that it did not belong there.)

- It's super easy to rearrange just one section if it needs a refresh.

- It makes sorting easy.

- It automatically keeps yarn quantities together.

- It's incredibly easy to add your latest fiber acquisitions to your existing stash without the slightest extra effort. New yellow yarn? Put it with the yellow yarn. Done!

- Of all the variety you may have in your stash (weight, fiber content, quantity), color variety is usually the most plentiful for the home yarn stasher.

Potential Disadvantages

- Yarn weights are mixed together. I don't mind this one bit, but if you don't have a lot of labels on your stash yarn and find it challenging to keep track of what's what, then mixing them all together might bother you.

- If most of your stash is multicolored—variegated, speckled and/or striped—then sorting by color could be tricky.

- If storing your yarn in a visible way isn't your cup of tea, sorting by color may not make much sense. This method works well when yarn is visible (such as in open shelving), but if you plan to store yarn in drawers or closets, it's not quite as meaningful.

- Storing yarn out in the open means you'll need to be consistent about keeping the space clean and doing regular stash reboots (which we'll talk about soon), but keeping things tidy and organized is important no matter how you sort and store your stash.

Category 2: Sorting by Weight

The other method that works well is to sort by yarn weight. This is a great system if you like to keep your yarn in drawers, totes or closets. It's also useful for those who like to knit from a wide range of yarn weights. Prior to my epiphany about my rainbow yarn cubes, sorting by weight had been my default, and it's the option that most yarn collectors try first.

Sorting by weight makes a lot of sense, and how you sort may have a lot to do with how visual you are. Some people love to see all the colors mixed together. Some people don't. The best way to find out how you feel about it is to give it a try and see.

"Out of sight, out of mind has been my nemesis! Now that I can see my stash—sorted by weight—it's easy to shop in it."

—BARB M., STASH SPRINT STUDENT

This method works especially well in a yarn shop, where you have a reasonably robust selection of yarn in every weight available. Yarn stores must appeal to a range of customers with different fiber interests. But the rest of us aren't obligated to buy a little bit of everything, so we stash the weights of yarn we like most. (Notice I didn't say "use" most, because, as you'll soon learn, we are likely to own all sorts of yarn we'll never use.)

Sorting by weight can, however, have mixed results, so it's important to make sure your stash has enough variety for this approach to work. If 90 percent of your stash is fingering weight yarn, then when the time comes to search for your next fingering weight project, you'll have to search through ALL the fingering weight yarn to find what you need.

Advantages

- Keeping the same weight skeins together makes it easy to mix and match different brands or colors for the same project.

- Storing by weight makes it easy to put away new purchases.

- You'll always know where to start when choosing yarn for a project.

- This is a great method for those who store their yarn in drawers, totes or other tucked-away places.

- It will automatically keep yarn quantities together, so skeins that are the same will naturally stay together.

- Variegated and speckled yarns are easy to store by weight, rather than having to worry about which color is dominant for a color sorting method.

Potential Disadvantages

- If you gravitate to just one or two favorite yarn weights, your collection may not have enough variety to warrant this method of organization. If you have far more of one weight than others, it may not feel very organized when it comes time to search for what you need.

- If you want to store yarn in open shelving where it's visible, sorting it by weight can look a bit cluttered.

- Yarn weight labels are not consistent. What may be called a "worsted weight" in one yarn, might be called "DK" in another. Even if you've sorted by weight, when the time comes to choose yarn for a project, you'll still have to dig through and compare the yarn in any particular weight category to find the ones that will work best together in a project. This is especially true if you're a sweater knitter, because even seemingly slight variations in weight can produce dramatically different results for fit and fabric.

Category 3: Sorting by Project

For those with a smaller stash who tend to shop for specific projects, you may prefer to sort by project rather than by weight or color. Keeping the pattern (and sometimes even needles) together with the yarn for a project is a handy way to create your own kits so they're ready to go when you are. Sorting by project shifts the process of "searching your stash" away from the hunt for yarn, and instead becomes a search for the next project. But as you consider this approach, ask yourself how often you follow through on your project ideas. Do you really make the project as is, or do you often end up using the yarn for another purpose?

A cautionary tale:

"A couple of years ago I started putting a lot of my yarn with the pattern I bought it for. I thought this was genius, but now I just have a bunch of bags with yarn in them."

— MONICA S., STASH SPRINT STUDENT

Monica's experience is not unique, which is why I don't advocate this method for most of my stash students. But if you like to stick to one project at a time, have very limited space or if you tend to plan (and stick to) your projects, even over time, this might be the right approach for you.

Advantages

- If you always shop with a plan and like to assign a specific project to every skein you bring home, sorting it with the pattern and project information can make it easy to grab and go when you're ready to get started.

- This system works well for small spaces.

- It's relatively easy to keep organized and maintained.

- It's simple to quantify how much room (and time) you have for more projects.

- If you're someone who likes to buy project kits, then you'll probably enjoy making your own.

Potential Disadvantages

- Assigning yarn to a project up front can be limiting and may be less inspiring.

- You may outgrow the pattern style or yarn before you get around to working on it or may end up using the yarn for something else.

- You are more likely to forget about the yarn you have on hand because it's already assigned to a specific project.

Choose One and Go

Choose the category that makes the most sense for now and dive in. You'll find out soon enough if it's not the right fit, and you can always switch gears if it doesn't work out the way you expect it to. Chances are you won't know how well it works until you try it.

This part of the process is an excellent excuse to turn on some happy tunes (or your favorite podcast), roll up your sleeves and get down to business. Sort your yarn into piles (or boxes or bags) based on the category you've chosen and keep sorting until every skein is accounted for. Don't forget your basket of leftovers or the bag of special yarn hiding in your bedroom closet.

Getting your yarn organized will feel a lot like a dance in the beginning, a few steps forward, a few steps back. Do you like the cha-cha? Great! This is basically a dance party.

Next stop, Containerville.

Containers: How to Store and Display Your Stash

The right containers make all the difference in how easy it is to keep your stash organized, but that doesn't mean you have to run out and buy a bunch of swanky new baskets to get the job done. You might already have what you need, so let's start with what you have and expand from there. In this section, we'll evaluate your container assets and how they work in your space so you can store your stash in a way that's easy to access and keep organized.

As you consider your containers, look for options that make it easier—not harder—to get to your yarn. If you can't see or find your yarn when you need it, you're a lot less likely to use it. It's as simple as that.

> *"Before this, my craft room was so packed with stuff I couldn't go in without cringing. Things in bags were forgotten because I hadn't opened some of them in years. I spent more time planning and rearranging yarn . . . than actually creating. I could never find what I was looking for and often pulled out a whole shelf of fiber to find something."*
>
> —CAMI O., STASH SPRINT STUDENT

What we've done so far is a great first step, but we're not all the way there yet. The right containers will make it easy to find what you're looking for so you can spend less time searching and more time knitting.

"The game changer for me was making my stash visible. Now when I'm tempted by a sale, I can easily look at what I have and know what I want. It's really easy to buy yarn, put it all away and forget you bought it . . . I find that I'm more likely to reach for [these] skeins because I see them out in the open all the time."

—ERICA E., STASH SPRINT STUDENT

A Container's Job

A container's job is to contain things, ideally in an organized and useful way. But anything can be a container: the shelf underneath your coffee table, the kitchen table, the hall closet. Just because it CAN hold yarn, doesn't mean it should. The secret to a good container is to make it as easy as possible to find what you need.

I first learned about the container concept from organizing guru and author Dana K. White, who rocked my world with her simple but powerful revelation that your home is a container. Your craft room is a container. Your shelf is a container. And when the container is full, it's full.

What you're about to do now is very different from any stash organizing you've done in the past; you're not just moving things around. You'll be assigning space to your yarn collection, assessing what you have and soon you'll be putting things back together in a way that makes your life easier.

Your Container Should Make It Easy to

- Know what you have
- Store what you use
- Buy what you need
- Stay organized

The most important thing about a container is that it defines the limits of your space. Space is finite, and if you want to stay organized, you can't just expand the boundaries of your stash until it takes over the house. Setting boundaries for where your stash lives can keep it from crowding out other spaces in your home and creating chaos and resentment—for you and for the others who live with you. Have you heard the adage, "Fences make good neighbors"? It applies here as well. Identifying the limits of your container will make it easier to enjoy your creative time, use your resources wisely and have clarity so you'll know when it's time to de-stash or go shopping.

Defining your container is making a commitment to yourself—it's a boundary. Without it, yarn can easily end up filling all the nooks and crannies of your home. (And it is frustratingly easy to hide, because it can squish into almost any spot.) And even if it's the exact same amount of yarn before and after you get it organized, the very act of putting it in order and setting boundaries makes the yarn you already have significantly more interesting. The right container makes your stash more useful, and it makes yarn-related decisions easier. *Does this new yarn fit into my container? No?* Then it's time to decide what has to go to make room for it. And if you're not willing to part with anything, you'd better knit (or crochet) a little faster to use up yarn and make space. Some of us take up a

secondary hobby like weaving or knitting machines to make it easier to use stash yarn quickly. If you have the space for one more thing and are committed to using your stash a little faster, it's worth considering. BUT adding more hobbies to the mix can also be a rabbit hole that makes things worse instead of better, so proceed with caution.

The goal is not to keep increasing the size of your container so you can buy more, but to let the container decide how much you can keep. If you're reading this, you've likely already tried the "more, more, more" approach, and while it surely isn't a bad thing to have more yarn, if you can't find it when you need it, then what's the point?

Remember the Assessing Your Fiber Real Estate exercise in Step One (pages 11–15)? The space in your home has value. Defining your yarn container is a way of being intentional about how much space your yarn is allowed to consume and how much real estate you're willing to devote to it. I used to feel a bit guilty buying new yarn when I still had plenty of perfectly good yarn at home, but once I defined my container and stuck to it, that boundary changed my approach. Instead of feeling guilty about new yarn, I'm simply keeping my inventory stocked.

My "container" is a series of cube shelves against the wall of my office, and every cube is currently full. In fact, I went on a shopping spree recently, and my containers couldn't handle everything I brought home, so I had to make decisions about which yarns were going to find a new home. I didn't give away anything precious, but I did give away perfectly good yarn that I might have used eventually. Maybe. But it's been on my shelf for years and it's not in a colorway that I would normally gravitate toward, so when push comes to shove, that's the yarn that gets liberated so it can live up to its potential with someone else.

Primary Containers vs. Secondary Containers

Your primary container will be the closet, room or the dresser you've chosen as the umbrella under which all the yarn you own will live. If you have a very limited amount of space, it might be a small rolling cart. Use what you have.

Start by identifying your primary container for your yarn collection. Your primary container will depend on your living area and how much space you can reasonably commit to the proper care and keeping of yarn. My primary container is a 100-square-foot (9-square-m) home office.

Secondary containers are much smaller. These are the tools you use to separate yarn into meaningful quantities and keep things organized: drawers, shelves, baskets, cubbies, dividers, etc.

So, in other words, I can't reasonably fill my entire office with yarn, because I also need room for a desk and office supplies, a few mannequins, lots of books, my project bag collection and my knitting machine (whose name is Daphne). I need to be able to work and access the space efficiently.

That's where secondary containers come in. You likely already have more than a few of these lying around. How you sort and store your yarn will dictate how easy it is for you to find and use what you have. Your mission is to choose containers that eliminate barriers and make your job easier. Barriers are the layers of effort that you must pass through to get to your yarn. Doors, lids, drawers and layers can all be barriers—the fewer, the better.

Before you run out to The Container Store® or IKEA for shiny new shelves and fancy baskets, consider your assets:

- How can you maximize the space you have?

- If floor space is limited, can you go vertical?

- Is there room in the margins (like narrow spaces next to shelves) where you could reasonably create additional space?

- Do you already have some things in your house that you can turn into yarn storage containers?

- Can you move things around or get rid of a piece of furniture to make it easier to organize your stash efficiently?

- Do you really need more containers, or do you just need to change the way you're using what you already have?

Getting organized doesn't have to be expensive. It'll take time and creativity, sure, but you probably already have things around the house that you can use to get your stash in order. Start with what you have, and only add new containers if you really need them. You won't know what will fit until you start putting it all away. It might seem backward to choose your container first, but it's a lot easier to set that boundary ahead of time.

Here are a few of my favorite container ideas, but consider this list a starting point because the possibilities are endless.

Shelves

The containers I use most are white, square, stackable, 3 x 3 cube shelves. I know I just said that it's not necessary to run out and buy new containers, but if you DO, this is where I would start. These shelves have been a game changer when it comes to helping me keep my stash organized and accessible, and they're my favorite. Each cube has 11 x 11 inches (28 x 28 cm) of usable space, and I can store a surprising amount of yarn in each one. Cube shelving is versatile enough that it can be stacked horizontally or vertically, allowing you to maximize space even in a relatively small room. When it comes to storing a lot of yarn in a small area, vertical shelving can be your best friend.

Open shelves are perfect for storing yarn where you can see it, and if you're sorting by color, you may love being able to see your stash out in the open. But open shelving is also a great foundation for a less visible approach, if you prefer to add collapsible organizers that fit perfectly into each shelf so you can store yarn in a more discreet way.

This type of shelving is usually easy to find at your local home improvement store, and it's not terribly expensive. Open shelving might not be the first place you'd think to start when it comes to getting organized, but it's shockingly easy to use. If you're used to storing yarn hidden away in totes, the transition to a visible stash is a dream. The fewer barriers between you and your yarn, the easier it is to use, and the more fun you'll have shopping your stash.

Bookshelves

A bookshelf can be a handy container for yarn storage, but any shelf wider, longer or taller than 12 inches (30 cm) is too large. Ideally, you want containers that let you store your yarn in a single, visible layer so that it's easy to use and access. Since most bookshelves are wider than 12 inches (30 cm) across, you'll need to look for containers that will allow you to divide each shelf into smaller sections of about 10 to 12 inches (25 to 30 cm) each so you can use the space efficiently.

Dressers and Drawers

Dressers, drawers, armoires and other furniture work great for storing yarn, and it's always a bonus if you already have one on hand. If you like to keep your stash relatively small and manageable, a single dresser can be the perfect container for the job. You can use the drawers to separate by color or yarn weight, and—if there's room—you can keep ongoing projects in their own drawer too.

Totes

Ah, the big plastic tote. It's the elephant of storage rooms everywhere, and the space hog of many closets. If you've tried organizing your stash (to no avail) with the help of giant plastic totes, you're not alone. It's what I used again and again (and again) until I finally realized that my stash and I were never going to be BFFs if I insisted on keeping it locked up inside a tower of totes. Any unfortunate yarn that found itself in one of the bottom totes was as good as dead to me for all the trouble it took to get to it.

Big plastic totes might seem like a good way to protect your stash, but here are a few unfortunate truths about storing yarn this way:

1. When yarn is harder to get to, you're less likely to use it. (I know I've said this already, but the fact that it's so incredibly simple makes it the easiest advice to ignore. I can't stress enough how important this is.)

2. Digging around a large tote creates tangles and causes partial skeins to unravel, making it feel more like you're digging around in a junk drawer rather than shopping your stash.

3. When yarn is out of sight and out of mind, it's more likely to become a victim of pests that take advantage of dark, unbothered areas. Yarn benefits from being squished and moved around frequently, and it not only reminds you what you have but makes it more difficult for pests to set up shop on your yarn shelves. The more accessible it is for you, the easier it will be to keep an eye on it.

4. Most large totes are for storage, not for things you want to be able to access on a regular basis.

If you really want to store your stash in plastic for safety purposes, skip the large totes and choose smaller plastic containers with clear sides. They should be large enough to contain at least one sweater's worth of yarn, but small enough that you can easily lift the lid and see what's inside without having to dig around or dump everything out. My ideal size is somewhere in the range of 12 inches (30 cm) wide, 12 inches (30 cm) tall and no more than 12 inches (30 cm) deep to make it easy to keep organized, and, ideally, store your skeins standing on end so you can see exactly what's inside.

Closets

Closets can be tricky, but they are a good option if you can bypass some of the more common closet pitfalls. First, it's easier to develop a tolerance to chaos because you can close the door when you don't want to look at it. Second, closets tend to encourage us to stack and layer things until they become difficult to access. A closet, in and of itself, is a primary container, so you'll still need a system for keeping things sorted INSIDE the closet. An ideal stash closet is one in which you can see your stash when you open the door and easily reach for what you need without having to unstack anything to get to it. Consider open shelving, hooks, carts and other organizers that allow you to eliminate barriers and ensure user-friendly access.

Hooks

If you're a multiple-project person (like me!), hooks are a great way to keep your current WIPs out of the fray, while making them easy to grab and go. And if you have a few cute project bags on hand, all the better! Keeping ready-to-go projects in a visible location isn't just cute but can also be practical in a crisis. One of my knitting students, Lee, took an unexpected trip to the hospital emergency room a few months ago, only to end up being admitted with a life-threatening issue. She left the house in such a hurry that she forgot to grab her knitting and ended up spending a week in the hospital without a project. There was no easy way to explain to her husband where to find the project she wanted. If she'd been able to say, "It's on the hook by my yarn shelf," he could have easily brought her what she needed. A series of hooks can be the perfect container for ongoing projects, and when the number of projects in progress outgrows the number of hooks you have, you'll know it's time to finish one before you start another.

Hot Tip: *While it's not essential to label your project bags, it's a nice way to keep track of projects when you're rotating between them. Anything you can do to make it easy to identify what's in the bag will be a time-saver when you're in a hurry.*

Coat-Tree

A simple coat-tree can be the perfect option for storing your project bags, even in a narrow space. In fact, a coat-tree can often fit into a space that might otherwise go unused. If you don't have the wall space for hooks or can't put holes in the wall because you're renting, a skinny coat rack is the next best thing. It'll allow you to use vertical space in an intentional way, and create meaningful use for marginal areas of a room. If you already have a plan for storing your WIPs, you can also use a coat-tree to hang empty project bags to make them easy to access when you're ready to start something new. A coat-tree also works well for hanging ready-made project kits if you've decided to categorize your stash by project.

Baskets

I grew up in a house that had baskets everywhere: on shelves, on the floor, in the bathroom and even on the walls. I thought baskets were a given in every home. But baskets, like yarn, can be a weakness, and it's easy to end up with far more than we can reasonably use.

Before you rush out for another adorable basket to organize your space, figure out exactly where you're going to put it and how you'll use it. Will it store yarn? If so, it should be tall enough to stand your skeins on end so you can see them. Remember, the size and shape of your container will either help or hinder your ability to access yarn. Choose baskets that are the right size and shape to make the best possible use of the space they're in. Every basket needs a specific job to do, or else it will take up space and collect clutter. Giant baskets might seem like a great idea for yarn storage, but they're tough to keep organized and will be perpetually messy. Small- and medium-sized baskets are best.

One of my favorite uses for baskets is to keep one in a visible place where I can put my latest yarn acquisitions. It's a nice way to extend the joy of bringing home new yarn and gives me time to savor them before I tuck them in place on my shelves.

Hot Tip: *You can also use baskets to store your grab-and-go project bags, keep your needles and hooks or hold blocking pins, tape measures and other notions.*

Odd Containers

Anything can be a yarn container if you really try, but my favorites are those that make the best use of space and can store a reasonable amount of yarn. Even containers meant for other things, like magazine organizers and new office-sized wastebins can be perfect for storing yarn if they fit your space. When you're out and about searching for containers, don't limit yourself to traditional storage systems. Consider the space you have and look for containers that fit. If it can hold yarn in a way that looks nice and makes it easy to access, it can be a container.

Working with a Small Space

If you're working with a small space or don't have a designated craft area in your home, a portable stash system might be the answer. A small rolling cart with shelves can serve as a mini-stash unit. Use it to store WIPs, yarn for your next projects, notions and more! Use every inch of space as carefully as you can. A rolling cart can fit into a small space, and it works well when you don't have a designated craft room and may need to move your supplies from one area to another (while still keeping them organized).

Effective use of space is a challenge we all face, but it IS possible to keep an extraordinary amount of yarn in a relatively small amount of space if you do it right. The goal is to use your resources to their fullest advantage. If all you have is a closet, use both the floor space AND the wall space. If you only have a dresser, use every drawer wisely.

Using the Right Tools for the Job

Look for storage solutions that can help you stay organized with the fewest possible barriers between you and your yarn. You don't have to keep it out in the open, but be cautious about anything that has you stacking multiple layers on top of each other. The more stacking and unstacking you'll have to do to access your yarn, the more frustrating it will be to use your stash.

Why keep a stash at all if it's easier to just buy new yarn rather than find the yarn that you know is in your home somewhere? There's nothing wrong with shopping for each project as it comes, and if that's your jam, go for it. (Although, there's something to be said for having the right yarn on hand for the emergency late-night cast-on . . .)

My friend Heidi usually doesn't stash more yarn than she needs for the next few projects, and while I'm pretty sure this approach would kill me, it works for her. My friend Erika and my sister Anna keep relatively robust amounts of yarn on hand and wisely work through both stash yarn and new yarn at a consistent pace. Do what works for you and adapt as needed.

Storage Tips

- Stacking yarn in single layers where all the ends are facing you (such as on a shelf) or standing your skeins on end (such as in a basket or drawer) will make it easier to shop your stash.

- Curtain rods mounted to the wall in your craft room or in a closet can be a great place to hang project bags and notion pouches.

- Wall hooks (typically for jackets) work great for hanging project bags with WIPs.

- Door organizers work well for hooks and needles, and I prefer to place them on closet doors rather than main doors (which get a lot more action opening and closing).

- Closet organizers can be a great way to store yarn out of sight but within easy reach.

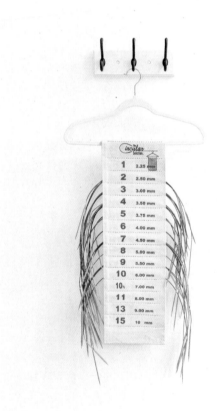

Taking Inventory

You've sorted your yarn and settled on your containers, but it's still not time to put it all away—not yet. This next step is an eye-opener, and it's one of the most satisfying parts of the process. By the time you finish this step you will know, yardage and all, what's in your stash, how much you have and how likely you are to use it. Hard to believe, right? But I have a secret weapon: a spreadsheet!

There's a big difference between yarn that you're **keeping** and yarn that you're **using**, and right now is the perfect time to assess both what you have and what you really use so you'll know what deserves space on your shelves. Let's face it: All yarn is useful, but not all of it will be useful to you. This is your chance to streamline the chaos-formerly-known-as-your-stash into the lovely, curated, soul-soothing collection you always knew it could be.

Asking the Fun Questions

The fun part of this process is playing with and inspecting all the yarn in your collection. After all, you're a fiber artist, so yarn squishing comes with the territory. You may think you already know what's in your stash, but I bet there are a few surprises hiding out in there. Taking an actual inventory is how you shed light on the situation so you can make a plan for moving forward. As you go through this process, here are the questions you'll be asking:

1. Who are you?
2. What are you made of?
3. Do we have a future together?

It's basically the dating game, but with yarn.

Create a spreadsheet like the one shown below and fill in the answers for every skein in your stash. Start with one pile at a time to make it manageable and fill in whatever details you have. It's okay to leave some areas blank if the yarn is missing a label. This is less about each individual skein and more about the big picture of what's filling up your fiber real estate. **This is one of the most time-consuming parts of the process, but don't skip it.** The results are worth it. Some of my students spent an entire weekend, or even a couple of weeks, documenting their stash, and how long it takes you will depend on the size of your stash and how much time you can spend on the project. I recommend giving yourself a nice reward when you reach the finish line. This is a labor of love, and you have definitely earned a treat. (If that treat is a new skein of yarn, make sure you put it on your spreadsheet.)

The good news is that your yarn is already out in the open and sorted into piles, so documenting what you have should be relatively easy. Put on your favorite show and multitask while you go.

Brand	Base Name	Weight	Yarn Type	Color Name	Color Description	Type	Yards	Grams	Number of skeins	Total Yardage
Appalachian Baby Design	Sport	Sport	cotton	Baby Silver	silver	solid	194	85	2	388
Appalachian Baby Design	Sport	Sport	cotton	cream	cream	solid	194	85	2	388
Ashford 8-ply	Tekapo	DK	New Zealand wool	gold	gold	solid	218	100	3	654
Berroco	Ultra Wool	DK	superwash merino	gold	gold	solid	292	100	1	292
Berroco	Ultra Wool	DK	superwash merino	hot pink	hot pink	solid	292	100	0.75	219
Brooklyn Tweed	Peerie	fingering	wool	Mesa	pink	tweed	210	50	2	420
Brooklyn Tweed	Shelter	worsted	wool	Embers	rust	tweed	140	50	2	280

"After taking time to sort and log my stash, I always go to that sheet first when I have a new pattern I want to make. Instead of yarn sitting around—and me spending hundreds of dollars on new yarn—I've been able to use stash yarn for two sweaters, a throw, a pair of mittens and a pair of socks this year already. Prior to this, I almost never used my stash yarn!"

—JOANNE G., STASH SPRINT STUDENT

Identifying What You Love (and Use)

Once you've finished documenting your stash, it's time to review your project history. This part will be especially telling. Bringing home yarn is the easy part . . . we could do that in our sleep. USING the yarn is a very different thing, and it may surprise you to see the difference between what you're stashing and what you're using. Knowing what you *really* use will make it easier to shop with your stash in mind.

"Because of this process, I have figured out what yarns I have too much of and which ones I don't have enough of based on what I routinely use and make."

—LEA D., STASH SPRINT STUDENT

You may need to step away from your stash for a bit and sit down with your computer for this part. Take a trip down memory lane and start writing down all the projects you remember working on for the last three to five years. Look through your pattern purchases, check your finished project photos and check your social media accounts to see which projects you've shared. If you keep leftovers from projects, look through your pile of oddballs to see if they trigger any memories about projects you may have forgotten. You will likely

have a few gaps in your memory, and that's okay. Just do the best you can. Create a second tab on your yarn catalogue spreadsheet called "Project History" and fill it in to the best of your ability, using the example below as a guide for how to set it up.

Project Type	Yarn Weight	Adult/ Child	Year	Finished?
Cardigan	Fingering	Adult	2023	Yes
Shawl	Fingering	Adult	2021	No
Pullover	DK	Adult	2022	Yes
Beanie	Sport	Child	2023	Yes

Review your yarn catalog and project history, and notice the following:

1. What have you been knitting or crocheting for the last twelve months?

2. How about the last two to three years?

3. Which types of projects are in your "to be made" queue?

4. Which projects did you think you'd be working on that haven't actually made their way to the top of your queue yet?

5. Which types of yarn do you gravitate toward?

6. Which yarns feel dated or don't appeal to you anymore?

7. Does anything in your stash make you cringe?

8. If you're keeping a lot of stash yarn with gift knitting in mind, how often are you actually knitting gifts?

9. How many projects have you started, but not finished?

10. Is there anything in your yarn inventory that surprises you?

Comparing what you're keeping with what you're actually using can make it easier to decide what should stay and what should go (which we'll cover in Step Four: Deciding What Stays [and What Goes] on page 49). My stash student Ashley discovered that more than 60 percent of her stash was filled with fingering weight yarn—a yarn weight she apparently loved to buy but didn't like to use. Imagine finding out that the reason you don't use your stash is because you're stashing all the wrong yarn! Here's what another student had to say about her own discovery:

"I realized that it is okay to acknowledge that I have changed as a knitter and that my yarn and pattern tastes have changed. I am proud of the fact that I am always growing and evolving as a person, so why wouldn't that growth impact my artistic expression? Gathering yarn that I know (if I am honest with myself) I will never knit with and gifting it to someone else was so freeing. I still have a lot of yarn, but it looks new and fresh, and I am excited to use it and shop from my stash! My personal stash vision is so much clearer!"

—SANDIE B., STASH SPRINT STUDENT

Several of my students noticed that their stash contained many sock-specific yarns, even though they no longer had any desire to knit socks. Or on the flip side, they had a ton of sweater quantities, and all they really wanted to knit anymore were socks and hats. My student, Barb, shared that she had a hefty amount of chunky weight yarn that she bought on sale, but she lives in a mild climate where heavy wool is rarely (if ever) wearable. Knowing what you have is one thing, but knowing what you USE is the real secret to a happy stash.

What are you learning about yourself and your stash as you work through this process? Have you had any AHA! moments that make you think differently about what you want to keep in your stash?

Stash Tip: *If you've discovered a surprising abundance of yarn or needles in a certain color or size, pay close attention: This might be a hint about your shopping autopilot. Autopilot purchases are what you buy when you know you need something, but you didn't bring a list and now you can't remember what you needed. There's a little trigger in the back of your brain that defaults to a safe purchase—something you know you'll use. This most often happens when your stash isn't organized and/or you're not shopping with a plan. The good news is that getting your stash under control will usually resolve this problem.*

Unfinished Projects

One more thing we should address before we move on is the burden of unfinished projects. Projects can linger for any number of reasons, but here are some of the most common:

- Your project may have gotten waylaid by an unexpected life event or trauma, and now when you pick it up to work on it, it's an unfortunate reminder of tough times. I have a gorgeous sweater in a basket that's 90 percent finished, but I was working on it when my dad passed away unexpectedly, and I still can't bring myself to finish it. Yarn has the potential for joy, but it can also hold on to our trauma. Sometimes finishing a project can be part of the healing process, and other times it might need to be tossed, frogged (ripped out) or even given away to someone else who might want to finish it. If you have a project like this, and it's been sitting dormant for more than five years, it might be time to let it go.

- Some projects aren't as much fun as we expect them to be. Maybe the pattern is fiddly, or the yarn is splitty or you realized you don't like the color. Maybe you've even changed your mind about which size to make but haven't been able to bring yourself to start over again. If you've halted work on a project because it's not bringing you joy, it's okay to be honest with yourself. Now is the perfect time to let it go. You can give it away, recycle the yarn or toss the whole thing away. It's up to you. Truth time: I've thrown away a perfectly good, half-finished sweater because I absolutely hated the yarn, and I wasn't happy with the sweater. Did I feel wasteful? Yes, but only for a minute. Once it was gone, I never thought of it again. Getting rid of dead weight feels so much better in the long run, and if the yarn is miserable to work with, it's not very nice to give it away and expect someone else to suffer through it.

- You started working on a baby sweater for little George several years ago (could it be ten years already?). "Little George" is now preteen George, and he wants a hoodie, not a baby cardigan. Either finish the sweater and save it for the next baby in the family, or pull it out and re-stash the yarn (see page 65 for tips on re-stashing yarn after you've used it). A growing child waits for no one.

- You're missing critical details like which size needles you were using or what size sweater you were making. We have ALL been a victim of our own memory failure when it comes to projects that got put away and forgotten. I once borrowed a pair of needles from a project that was sitting in my closet and slid the stitches onto another random needle for safekeeping. Two years later, I grabbed the project bag to take with me to a retreat, and I just pulled it

out and started knitting. Did I remember that the size 5 needles on my project were NOT the needles I'd actually been knitting with? Nope. I had knit the first half of the scarf with size 7 needles and the second half with size 5. Imagine my surprise when I finally looked closely at my work only to realize that the second half of the scarf was dramatically smaller than the rest. If you're holding on to multiple projects that are missing critical details to allow you to finish, take the lessons and let the projects go. First, if you don't know what size you were making or needles you were using, you won't know in two more years, either. Second, remember to always keep a note with your project so you'll remember the needles and size details to save yourself the same headache later. We always think we'll remember, or we assume it'll only be in time-out for a little while. But friend, we won't remember, and projects sitting in time-out can end up there for YEARS.

Needles and Notions

Don't forget needles and notions! It's important to consider where your needles, hooks, tape measures, stitch markers and other gadgets will live in your stash so they're easy to access when you need them. Without a designated home, these seemingly small items can turn into a real hassle.

There are countless needle and hook cases available these days, but my favorite is the kind that hangs on the wall so I can see my needles at a glance. (I'm sure you can see the trend here. Visible = accessible!) As someone who knits a little each day, I like having quick access to my tools without having to search for them. Better still, having my needles in an easy, visible (but well-organized) location also makes it faster to put them away when I'm finished. Sometimes the biggest clutter culprit isn't the mess we make when we're looking for things, but the mess we leave when we set things down rather than putting them away. (As someone who is often guilty of this, I've had to train myself to put things directly in their home, rather than setting them down on a clean surface.)

If you're someone who knits or crochets every day, then you'll probably benefit from having your needles and notions easily accessible and out in the open. Otherwise, you may be fine keeping your supplies in a closed case, drawer or other container out of sight.

Bags

If you're a project bag collector like me (and a few thousand other knitters I know), you'll have to account for the bags in your stash as well . . . and not just the bags with projects in them, but all of the bags you've been collecting over the years. Bags are my weakness and, try as I might, I'm incapable of saying no to just one more. Unfortunately, my desire for more bags and the amount of space I have to store said bags are not one and the same.

Realistically, you DO need more than one or two bags on hand to account for multiple ongoing projects and/or choose the right size bag for whatever you're making. Some crafters like to match their bag to their project (how fun!), and as long as you're actively using your bag collection, having a variety of sizes and colors makes sense. However, if you're struggling to keep them organized and find that you're really only using a few of them, make a pile of the bags you're not using so you can consider whether or not they're worth keeping.

Deciding What Stays (and What Goes)

You've dumped, sorted and containerized. You've taken inventory, and you've figured out what you really use. Now it's time to make peace with everything you love and everything you don't. This part is my favorite. It's time to put everything you've learned to use, finally fill up those shelves, and let your containers help you make decisions along the way.

Making the Hard Decisions Easy

As you start putting things away, it's important to separate the keepers from the . . . *not keepers*. All yarn is useful, but not all of it is useful to you. Inevitably, some of it is clutter disguised as yarn. But even when you know that's the case, it's not always easy to let it go.

The yarn you don't (and won't) use will become a burden that will weigh you down with guilt and overwhelm you every time you deal with it. Chances are you already know what that feels like.

"Organizing was tough! All that yarn! All that money! Understanding that I was never going to use it was hard to admit. Thanks to [this process] I was able to give myself permission to let it go, and now my shelves make me happy!"

—TAMI D., STASH SPRINT STUDENT

Pruning Makes Room for More

We have several apple trees espaliered—or trained to grow along a horizontal trellis—down the length of our driveway. At the end of each growing season, the trees are pruned back (rather dramatically) to keep them neatly contained and to encourage fruit production in the fall. Every year I'm astonished by the number of apples we're able to grow in such a small space, and it wouldn't be possible without careful, consistent pruning. Yarn may not spontaneously fill our shelves on its own (if only!), but there's something to be said for making room so that new resources and ideas have somewhere to grow.

Keeping your stash organized requires pruning away the parts that are no longer serving your creativity. Don't beat yourself up for buying yarn that turned out to be a dud. (We've all done it.) I've wasted good money on yarn that I didn't like using or that wasn't quite the color I thought it was when I ordered it online. I would rather cut my losses and share it with someone else than kick myself for making a mistake. It happens to the best of us. Pruning creates space for more: more creativity, more ideas and yes, *more yarn*. If your stash is always bursting at the seams, there will never be room for more.

One of my stash students, Susan, had a game-changing epiphany about letting go of some of her yarn:

"I realized it's not about what I'm letting go. It's that I get to decide what will stay. That makes the decision so much easier."

What Gets to Stay?

Most unwanted things are relatively easy to toss or give away when they're broken or no longer needed. Yarn is different. When the yarn in your stash is perfectly good, logic tells us that we should keep it. It's useful, desirable (to someone) and probably still in like-new condition. Why would we get rid of something that is still perfectly good and useful?

The reality is that few of us have unlimited time or space. There are only so many free hours for knitting or crocheting, and only so much space that we can reasonably dedicate to yarn storage. Here are a few things to consider:

- Does it make sense to use your limited space to store more yarn than you could ever use in your lifetime?

- Wouldn't it be nice to be able to find the yarn you want without having to dig through the piles of OTHER yarn that you don't particularly like?

- Negative energy blocks creativity. If anything in your stash is there because of guilt or obligation, it does not belong there. You will feel freer and more inspired when you let it go.

For any yarn you may still be hesitant to let go, ask yourself the following:

1. Do I like this yarn? If so, why am I not using it?

2. Is there something about this yarn that bothers me? Is it the fiber content? Is it splitty? Does it feel rough in my hands? Is there something about the texture I don't like? (And is the issue likely to improve if I just save it a little longer?)

3. Do I like the color? Is it a color I would normally use? If yes, then why haven't I used it before now?

4. When is the last time I worked with this yarn weight? What makes me think I might use it at some point?

5. Do I feel inspired when I look at this?

6. Can I think of at least two projects off the top of my head that I would consider making with this yarn?

7. Am I keeping this yarn out of guilt or obligation? What advice would I give to my dearest friend if they were in my shoes? (Sometimes we give our friends better advice than we give to ourselves.)

8. If I had been given this yarn for free with no strings attached, would I mind getting rid of it? (Sometimes it helps to take the dollar amount and obligation off the table so we can see how we really feel about something.)

9. Would I pay full price to buy this yarn again today? (If you're anything like me, you've probably purchased more than a few sale skeins that you wouldn't have bought at full price. Sale skeins are frequently the ones that sit in our stash the longest.)

10. How long has this been sitting in my stash?

11. What has it cost me to store this yarn over the years? (Look back at the Your Yarn Square Footage exercise [page 14] if that will be helpful!) How much longer does it deserve to take up space in my home?

Here's what some of my students have said about the experience of letting go:

"Now that I've started [organizing] I can't stop! It is so freeing, and it feels good to get out from the heavy load of the stash I have. So much of it I will truly never use, and it feels good to release that yarn [so I can] organize the yarn I have."

—SANDIE B.

"[This process] just confirmed what I already knew—my yarn stash was out of control! This has allowed me to be honest about how much my knitting has changed and given me the freedom to pass on the yarn I no longer want. I'm allowing myself to cherish the knitter I was in the past and celebrate the knitter I've become."

—TAMI B.

"Taking the time to look through each piece and deciding if I will actually use it was quite liberating!"

—GAY S.

The first time through your stash overhaul, you may not be ready to get rid of everything that really needs to go. That's okay; it's not a one-and-done process. Your priorities—and your stash—will change over time. Your container is your guide. If it fits, and you want to keep it, go for it. If it doesn't fit, then use what you've learned so far to decide what should stay and what should go.

Sunk Cost Bias

It's not unusual to get stuck thinking about how much you paid for the yarn. Good yarn isn't cheap. Even cheap yarn isn't cheap! But no matter how much you spent on it, it's impossible to use it if you can't get to it. Having too much of the wrong yarn makes it tough to stay organized, and it's much harder to shop your stash when you can't find anything. And if that's not a waste of money, I don't know what is.

> *"I have learned that it's okay to let go of yarn that I've just been holding on to because of the money . . . someone else can enjoy it, and I don't have to feel bad for letting it sit around."*
>
> —MARY R., STASH SPRINT STUDENT

The yarn that stays should be the yarn you'll realistically use—or at least expect to use—in coming years. If you don't love the color, if it carries the weight of obligation or guilt, if you just don't like it, *let it go.* Send it off with your blessing, and trust that the Fiber Fairies will find it a new happy home. Don't dwell on how you got here. Focus on the peace of mind you'll have going forward.

Do not—I repeat—**do not** try to make your container bigger just because you don't want to get rid of anything. If anything, double-check that you are using your containers in the most efficient way. (There's nothing wrong with going vertical so you can fit more yarn!) If it's organized and easy to access, go for it! Maximize the space you have. But at the end of the day, you'll know when you've tapped out your storage capacity. Remember that the goal isn't to find a way to keep it all; your goal is to **keep what you love and make it easy to use.**

Pack, Drop and Run

When you've determined what should stay, it's time to let go of what no longer belongs. This is your "pay it forward" (or PIF) pile. Sometimes reframing things in terms of what it will do for others can make it easier to feel good about the decision to let a few things go. Getting rid of old, yucky yarn is easy. It's letting go of the good stuff that can be difficult. But if you think of it as paying it forward so that someone else can have the thrill of using it, you can pack a lot more joy into the experience. Paying it forward means we're giving something of value so that someone else can benefit.

What Not to Keep?

- Anything that makes you cringe. (I don't care how expensive it was.)

- Yarn in colors you don't like.

- Yarn that has proven to be splitty or frustrating to work with. You may be tempted to save this kind of yarn for classes, but I've found that splitty yarn makes a technique class super frustrating. Use the good stuff and let this go.

- Yarn that you feel obligated to keep but don't like. Don't let someone else's yarn burden be your burden. You'll feel 1,000 times lighter when you kiss it goodbye.

- Yarn you've been holding on to for a decade and have never once considered for a project. If it hasn't been in the running for a project by now, things aren't looking good for it down the road.

- Anything that you don't enjoy working with (even if it's perfectly good yarn).

- Tiny bits and pieces of yarn that are too small to realistically use for a project. Are you REALLY going to use them? Probably not. Save your favorites in a decorative vase; gift them to the library, senior center, YMCA or preschool; donate them to a thrift store; or toss them in the wastebin. No one wants to throw away perfectly good yarn (and we certainly wouldn't admit it if we did), but if you can't think of anyone anywhere that would use it, does it really make sense to let it take up space?

Make the decision about what stays and what goes as quickly as you can, and then act on it. The longer you drag it out, the harder it will be. I make every effort to take my PIF pile right out to my car and deliver it to the new recipient within a day or two so that it doesn't sit. And if someone offers to come pick it up, make sure to pin down a date and time **in the very near future**—and include a caveat that if they don't pick it up that day, you'll donate it elsewhere. As much as you want the yarn to go to your #1 choice of new home, the more important thing is to get it OUT of yours. Do whatever it takes to rehome it before you change your mind. Once it's gone, you won't miss it.

"I think realizing that it's okay to rehome yarn has been quite helpful. [This process] has made me look hard at what I buy. Do I want to house it, or can it be available to the next knitter? I'm happier to have more space and a better idea of what I have."

—CHRISTINE M., STASH SPRINT STUDENT

"I felt guilty to get rid of these but after [working through] the different steps of stash-busting, I feel a sense of liberation already!"

—MARY N., STASH SPRINT STUDENT

A Few Ideas for Rehoming Yarn (the Easy Way)

- Gift the yarn to a friend in your knitting group or guild. Someone with a smaller stash might be thrilled for the boost. Fill those extra project bags that you no longer need with giftable yarn. Imagine what a treat this will be for the one who receives it!

- Take your PIF pile to your next knit night or guild meeting and offer it up for free to anyone who wants something, and then donate whatever remains to your local thrift store.

- Donate your stash to a senior center to provide projects for those who may not have the resources for new supplies.

- Donate your stash to a women's shelter, preschool or after-school program.

- Donate your stash to a church or charity that creates items for donations. **Tip:** Check first to see which yarns they can use before you donate. You don't want to make your problem someone else's problem.

Rehoming Yarn (the Hard Way)

- List your giveaway yarn for trade in a knitting or crochet forum.

- Sell your yarn online or at a local event.

The problem with trying to sell or trade your PIF pile is that it can take a lot of time with little reward. More likely than not, this same yarn will still be sitting in your stash six months from now. I understand the desire to get a return on your investment, but remember, too, the value of your time and peace of mind, not to mention your physical space. Shelves and closets are premium real estate in your home, and the cost of keeping yarn adds up. Wouldn't you rather use that space for yarn you love?

Whatever you do, don't bequeath the entirety of your PIF pile to someone else without first checking to see if they need it and have room for it. If they agree to take it, make sure you give it freely with no strings attached. Remember that even fabulous yarn can be a burden if it comes with a guilt trip, so gift your PIF pile without expectation and let the recipient do what they want with it. You will be liberated from the yarn that was weighing you down, and the recipient will have the freedom to use it joyfully and without pressure.

Now pack up that PIF pile and wish it well. Send it off to greener pastures with new opportunities. Also, don't panic, and please stick with me. There's a joyful, abundant stash on the other side of this journey, and you can do this. So, let's keep going.

Shopping Smart

If the process of curating my stash has taught me anything, it's that buying yarn is intrinsically connected to how we use it. It should be more than a decoration and more than mere closet insulation. I've heard it declared that buying yarn is its own hobby, and while I understand the sentiment, I respectfully disagree. Buying yarn for the sake of buying yarn is how we end up overwhelmed. I want to feel happy and inspired when I look at my stash. Don't you?

The problem really isn't that we all have too much yarn. I mean, sure, some of us may always keep more yarn that we can realistically use in a single lifetime (guilty as charged). But if we buy what we'll use, and we store it in a way that makes it easy to find, keeping a healthy yarn stash is a very practical thing to do.

Getting your stash in order is the first step, but it's not the finish line. There will be new projects, new shopping trips, new fiber festivals and new yarn clubs that you will not be able to resist. The good news is that you don't have to resist them. You just need a plan.

"When I shop for yarn, I'm more thoughtful about what I already have and how these new skeins will enhance my stash. I also realized that I need to buy in a quantity that will allow me to make what I want!"

—CHRISTINE M., STASH SPRINT STUDENT

Getting off the Yarn Diet Wagon

Yarn diets don't work—plain and simple. Yes, you can absolutely tell yourself that you're not allowed to buy any new yarn until you've knit through your stash, but then your stash becomes a punishment rather than a delight. I don't want the act of shopping my stash to feel like penance for bad buying decisions. I would rather stash wisely so that there's always a nice balance of both new and less-new yarn flowing through my projects. And if there are times when I need to exclusively shop my stash for a while, no problem! When you treat your stash like your own personal yarn shop, you'll feel abundant and grateful rather than limited.

When you buy the right yarn, you'll use it. There's nothing that feels better than shopping in your own stash and finding exactly what you need for a project. Instead of guilt and shame, you feel . . . dare I say it? Proud. A well-curated stash makes you feel like a smart cookie. Say someone asks, "Do you really NEED more yarn?" you can say, "Why, yes. Yes, I do. My stash is short on blue fingering weight skeins, so I most certainly DO need this." Getting organized gives you permission to go shopping because you know exactly what you need.

> *"[This process] has given me permission to buy yarn because I know what I have and what I don't have."*
>
> —KATHLEEN L., STASH SPRINT STUDENT

I would rather buy what I need than fill my space with yarn I won't use, wouldn't you? I can always tell when I bring home yarn that doesn't belong in my stash because I can't find a place for it, and it often ends up staying in the bag for weeks (or months) while I "think about" where it should go. I wish I could say that I don't still make that mistake sometimes, but I do—just

not as often as I used to. Impulse buying feels good in the moment, but smart buying feels good the whole way through.

> *"This has given me a new appreciation for what I already own. Prior to this, each time I contemplated a new project, I automatically shopped for yarn. But now my eyes are opened to what I already own. This has allowed me so much freedom! I know instantly what I have . . . and buy only what will enhance what I already have at home. I make it a point to shop my stash first. It really saves the knitting bucks!"*
>
> —NYDIA H., STASH SPRINT STUDENT

Impulse purchases do sometimes work out, and I'll never tell you that you can't just buy yarn in the moment because it feels right. Sure, go for it. Just be willing to give it away sooner than later if you realize you're never going to use it. Your impulse buy could be the perfect skein that someone else has been searching for. Whatever you do, don't hold on to mistake-yarn just to punish yourself. It won't do any good, and keeping it a little longer won't make you any more eager to use it. Never use your stash to punish yourself—that is not the kind of energy that leads to a happy project. It just makes you feel bad.

Adopting a Shopping Strategy

Remember that having a robust stash is a good thing, as long as you have room for it and you're storing what you'll use. Actively shopping for your stash is a good thing, and it will ensure that you have the right inventory for the projects in your queue. Trust me when I say that there is nothing better than being able to start a spontaneous project on a Saturday night because you had exactly what you needed in your stash.

"I've always been pretty organized with my yarn, but this has made me a better yarn shopper/collector. I have realized what yarn I like to use, what projects I like to knit and I no longer buy impulse yarn that I'll never use."

—GILDA E., STASH SPRINT STUDENT

But there are a few things to keep in mind if you want to keep your stash headed in the right direction:

1. **Buy what YOU love, not what others talk you into.** At the end of the day, you know what you love better than anyone else. If you're on the fence about a yarn purchase, hold off until you know it's what you want. Yarn that doesn't fit your interests will make more work for you down the road, as it takes up space that you could devote to yarn you'd much rather have. As soon as that yarn comes in the door, you'll have to figure out what to do with it. Remember: The wrong yarn will be a burden that you'll have to deal with later.

2. **Buy with project quantities in mind.** I've heard so many yarn stashers mention that they would love to use their stash, except they mostly knit sweaters and there are no sweater quantities in their stash. Friend, buy in quantities you'll use. Jot down the yardage you used for your last few projects and keep those as a ballpark figure when you're shopping without a specific project in mind. You don't have to use the yarn for exactly the pattern you envisioned, but at least you'll have enough for a realistic project.

"I've learned how to buy yarn so that I don't have all the one-skein wonders. As much as I love to buy yarn, I found that I was not loving my growing stash with no purpose and not enough time to use it."

—SUE M., STASH SPRINT STUDENT

3. **Buy solid and tonal colors to round out your stash.** If multicolor yarns are your jam, be sure you're also stashing solid and tonal colors that you can partner with them for projects. The one complaint I've heard most often from my stash students is that they want to use their stash, but they don't have the right yarns to go with anything. A curated stash means shopping with the whole stash in mind. What does your stash need for balance? What is it missing? What do you have too much of?

"My approach to yarn has completely changed. No longer do I just pick up one random skein of crazy yarn. I realize I want to have more solid/tonal colors, and I want sweater quantities!"

—TAMI B., STASH SPRINT STUDENT

4. **Be willing to learn as you go.** One of the most interesting things about curating your stash is learning from your own past and present behavior. As weird as it sounds, our buying habits don't always match our preferences. I've met many knitters who stash yarn they found on sale or they bought to support a small business, but the yarn itself isn't the kind of thing they would actually use. Curating your collection allows you to figure out what you really like and use so you can shop smarter when the time comes.

5. **Course-correct quickly.** Let go of the idea that you can't get rid of something because you bought it recently or spent a lot of money on it. Yes, you can get rid of it. And if you know it was a mistake, find your way forward as quickly as possible. Don't hold on to something you don't really want, no matter how recently you bought it.

6. **Shop sales carefully.** Sales are a godsend if you're a maker on a budget. But sale baskets are notorious for coaxing you into buying yarn you won't use just because the price is right. Most of my stash mistakes were skeins I bought on sale because I was so excited about the price that I forgot to check to see if it was yarn I would really use. Sale prices make it easier to justify yarn that we shouldn't be looking at in the first place. *But what if I decide to make green camo legwarmers someday? This drab, furry green yarn would be perfect, and it's 50-percent off!* You don't know a single person who wears legwarmers, much less camo ones. Step away from the green fuzz. When you're contemplating a yarn sale, don't bring it home unless the following two criteria are met:

A. Can you think of at least two specific, realistic projects you would make with this yarn?

B. Would you still want this yarn if it was full price?

If the answer to one or both of these questions is no, then keep walking.

"I've found that I'm now a much less spontaneous yarn shopper. I know what I have and what I like to knit with . . . Now when I buy, it isn't an impulse decision."

—GAY S., STASH SPRINT STUDENT

7. **Know what you have and what you use.** If you keep your stash where you can see it, you'll have a pretty good mental picture of what you have on hand already, but it doesn't hurt to snap a picture of your shelves before you shop. If you prefer to keep your stash tucked out of view, be sure you have your spreadsheet (page 42) on hand so you can refer to it when you shop.

8. **One skein, two questions.** If you are in the mood for an impulse buy and don't want to worry about a plan, I like to use the "one skein, two questions" rule. Choose the skein you can't live without and then ask yourself:

- Is there enough to make a hat?
- Who would wear it?

Hats are quick to make, don't require a lot of yarn and make perfect gifts. As long as you have enough to make a hat, and can think of someone who might want to wear it, go for it. (You don't even have to actually use it to make a hat, but at least you know you could.)

Adopting a shopping strategy will make it easier to stay organized over time. You'll be able to shop with confidence and clarity because you know exactly what your stash needs.

Creating Your Personal Yarn Shop at Home

Shopping your stash should be a delightful experience, marked by the satisfaction of having a curated collection that is both practical and beautiful. It won't happen overnight, but as you shop FOR your stash (not just IN your stash), you'll begin to build a collection that supports and inspires your creativity, no matter what it is you want to make. A curated stash is one that's been thoughtfully selected, organized and looked after so that it can do the job you've paid for it to do. In this section, we'll talk about how to continue to curate your collection over time and add the personal touches that will turn any simple yarn space into your very own personal yarn shop at home.

Curating Your Collection

We've talked about this already, but it's helpful to remember that the reason most of us haven't loved shopping our stash over the years is twofold:

1. It rarely had what we were looking for, and if it did, we might have been hard-pressed to find it.

2. Shopping our stash usually meant digging around in totes and bags that were hiding in inconvenient places. Talk about frustrating!

But now you know what you have, AND you know where it is. You also know what you like to work with, and what you love to make. And best of all, you've released the yarn you don't love to create a little space for what's next. (Or at least I hope you have.) The foundation is there, and now you just need a few little details to make your fiber nook complete.

Curation is the process that will allow your stash to grow with you as your creative journey expands and changes over time. Think of yourself as the owner of your very own personal yarn shop, because really, that's exactly what you are. What kind of shop would you like it to be?

I've filled my yarn space with my own curated collection of favorite yarn and added charming details that make the space feel cozy and inspiring. I have sheep-inspired art on the wall and a tiny handknit alpaca that was sent to me by a friend. I have a fun, sweary mug that holds my pens and double-point needles. I have a whiteboard where I write a little thought for the week. I use swatches from my favorite projects as coasters and, since I have a couple of nice windows in the space, I also keep two of my favorite plants in them. I have mannequins wearing my latest

projects and my favorite bags hanging on the door-knob. I treat my space like it's my yarn shop, even though the only person that shops there is me and the inventory is already paid for.

> *"I love going to Betty's Boutique (my stash) to shop for my next project. So far this year I've used stash to knit not one, but three sweaters and some cowls!"*
>
> —SUE M., STASH SPRINT STUDENT

What's in Your Shop?

Every yarn shop has its own character. Some are homey, while others are minimalist and modern. Some shops are a rainbow of color and gadgets and all the lovely stuff that'll put a spring in your step and inspire your daydreams. Some are filled to the brim, while others are sparse. Every shop has its own vibe, and your personal stash does too. It's time to be loud and proud of your yarn collection and give it the attention it deserves.

Being practical and organized is important, but why not borrow a few ideas from your favorite shop, whether it's your local store or one that you discovered on a vacation? Sure, you already bought the yarn, but your stash will be coaxing you to come back to it for a future project, and there's no reason you can't make that experience feel like a treat.

Yarn shops aren't only the suppliers of our yarn inventory; they're also a fabulous source of inspiration. If you need a few ideas to spice up your space, consider this your permission slip for a field trip. Visit a shop or two and see what they inspire. And if you need to grab a little extra yarn while you're there, be sure to read Step Five: Shopping Smart (page 57) first so you can shop with intention.

Things to Notice at Your Local Yarn Shop

1. How do they organize and store yarn?

2. How do they display needles? Bags? Patterns?

3. Do they have any unique kinds of art or display fixtures?

4. Do they use any unusual kinds of furniture or home accessories in their shop? (I once saw a yarn store that used an old card catalog from a library to sort needles. You never know what kind of discoveries you might make!)

5. Does the shop feature little extras like sassy magnets, handknit critters, funny sayings, fancy light fixtures or unique bookends?

6. Do they have rotating holiday displays?

7. How do they show off project inspirations?

8. Be sure to buy something on your visit (even if it's small) to thank the shop for being there.

Hot Tip: *Yarn shops often name their mannequins and dress them in actual clothes, and you can too! I have several dress forms now, but my favorite is called Betty White, and she wears a white dress that I bought on vacation and can no longer fit into.*

Frogging, Re-Stashing and Ongoing Projects

Creating your own personal yarn shop at home means having a range of yarn options for a single project so if one idea doesn't work out, you can quickly start again with something else. But you may find yourself halfway through a sweater or shawl before you realize that the yarn and pattern just aren't getting along. If this happens, it's not a big deal. Most yarn can be repurposed. (I say "most" because there's the occasional lace weight mohair that may try to fight back.) If you re-stash it in good shape, it'll be ready to go next time you'd like to use it.

Working with Frogged Yarn

Frogging (we call it this because you "rip it, rip it") the yarn (or pulling it out) is generally quick and easy to do, but working with that same yarn again can be a challenge, depending on the condition it's in. If you've just recently started knitting, you may be able to wind the yarn back up and reknit or crochet it again right away. But if it's been in the project for a while—or perhaps even been finished and blocked—you may have a very curly pile of yarn on your hands. Working with frogged yarn can affect your gauge and may produce uneven stitches. But good news! There are steps you can take to return your fiber to like-new condition so you can re-stash it for a future project.

Here are two methods I use to restore frogged yarn to its former glory. Keep in mind that your fiber content will affect your results, so some experimentation may be necessary to achieve the end product you want.

Small-Scale Yarn Restoration

If you've pulled out just a few yards of yarn to fix a section of your work and would like to be able to knit with it again quickly, try using a flat iron hair straightener. This method works best for animal fiber and should not—under any circumstances—be used with acrylic or acrylic blends. Acrylic yarn will melt. To see if this is a good choice for the specific fiber you're using, try it in a small section before you commit.

Set your flat iron to medium temperature. My rule of thumb is to use the same temperature that I would use for my own hair. Hold the yarn in front of you so that the loose strand is hanging down toward the floor, and gently place the flat iron about 12 inches (30 cm) away from the end so that the strand of yarn is sandwiched between the iron paddles. Slowly draw the iron down as you pull the yarn strand upward to create consistent heat as the flat iron glides down toward the end of the strand. Don't let the iron sit too long in any one spot. If the strand isn't quite as smooth as you want it to be, repeat this process along the same stretch of yarn. Work in 12-inch (30-cm) sections until you've smoothed the yarn and are ready to work with it again.

This can be a tedious process if you need to restore more than a few yards, but it works beautifully if you just need to smooth a small section so you can get back to your project.

Full Skein Restoration

If you're frogging large sections of yarn or full skeins, you'll want to give the yarn the full spa treatment. This process assumes you have already pulled out your project and have wound the frogged yarn into a ball or cake as a starting point. If you haven't done so, start there and come back to this process when you're ready.

You'll need:

- A yarn swift
- Small strands of yarn to tie the hank
- A clean basin
- Lukewarm water
- Softening fiber wash
- A clothes hanger

Set up your yarn swift, if you have one. If you don't, ask someone to assist you so you can wind it around their arms, instead. Wind the yarn completely around the swift until you have one large "hank" of fiber. **Note:** If you're familiar with using hand-dyed or small-batch yarn that comes in hanks, you'll recognize this process as the reverse of what you'd normally do with yarn. Instead of winding a loose hank into a ball, you're winding a ball back into a hank.

Use four or five small strands of extra yarn (ideally in a different color so you can easily see them) to loosely tie around sections of the hank. If in doubt on how to do this, you can see an example on nearly any hand-dyed skein of yarn. This step will keep the yarn from becoming a tangled mess as you proceed. Trust me on this one.

Once you've secured your hank with several ties, remove it from the swift and place it into a clean basin with lukewarm water and a softening fiber wash. Lukewarm water will be more effective than cold water, and softening fiber wash, although not critical, can help relax the fiber for added support. Let the hank soak in the water for 30 minutes. Don't rush this process. Some fiber will be stubborn (especially plant-based fiber), and the longer soak will make all the difference.

When your soaking time is complete, drain the water and press out as much excess water as you can. This next step is something I like to do outside, but you can make it work wherever you are. Place the damp hank around the top of a hanger so that it hangs straight down, allowing gravity to assist with the smoothing process. Place your hanger in an area with good airflow until the yarn dries completely. (I typically let mine

air-dry outside on a covered patio so that it's safe from sun, rain and birds.) When your hank is dry, you can twist it back into a skein or put it back on your swift to wind into a ball or cake.

Re-Stashing: Cakes or Skeins?

If you're planning to re-stash your frogged yarn, it's best to twist it back into a hank (when possible), especially if you're not planning to use it right away. This is not to say that you can't store cakes or balls of yarn and use them at a future date, but whenever possible, I like to leave my yarn in the skein because it's easier to store. Keeping yarn as close as possible to the original format will help retain its original shape while it's stored. If you do like to wind yarn into cakes for storage, be careful not to wind them too tightly as this can stretch out the strands and may affect your gauge while working with it.

Don't forget to hold on to your labels and keep them with the re-stashed yarn. It may be hard to remember the details from one yarn to another, and the labels will save time and guesswork.

Ongoing Projects

Not every lackluster project is destined to be frogged. Some just need a little time-out. Before putting your WIP on the shelf for an extended stay, be sure to include a note to let yourself know the pattern name, needle size and yarn you used, along with any extra notes about the pattern that you may want to remember when you return. Make sure to include your gauge, especially if it's different from the recommended pattern gauge, along with any modification notes. If possible, it's helpful to include a paper copy of the pattern with your progress clearly marked. If you're working from a book or digital copy, make sure to jot down any necessary details in a note to yourself so you'll be able to find your spot again.

Keeping Things Tidy (and Safe) Over Time

The first time through your stash is always the hardest. It's likely the first time you've honestly confronted every single skein of yarn, held it in your hands and consciously decided to let it stay or not. If you implement even just a portion of what you learn in this book, your future stash reboots will be easier and easier each time. It doesn't have to be perfect, but if you show up and try your best, you'll never have to start back at square one ever again.

One of the benefits of organizing your yarn by color, weight or project is that you can easily spot organize just one section of your stash whenever you have a little extra time. If the bin of blue yarn is looking a little messy, empty it out and give it a little refresh. Look for anything that might be out of place or need to join the next PIF pile. If you've organized your stash by project, keep eyes on what you have and make sure those projects still sound like a good idea. Tidy up loose yarn and restack everything neatly where it belongs. Spot organizing makes it easy to stay on top of your stash and can keep things from spiraling out of control.

Refreshing Your Stash with the Seasons

The more I organize and reorganize my stash, the more I enjoy doing it. Think of it as your annual inventory. It's satisfying to spend time squishing yarn and putting things back where they belong, and it's reassuring to see that things are in order. Your stash is an investment, and an annual stash reboot is your audit process to check in on your investment and make sure everything is as it should be. Yarn that is regularly moved around and squished is less likely to become the victim of moths, mice or other creepy-crawlies.

At least once a year, I schedule time to empty my shelves and sort everything again from top to bottom. I donate a few new things that don't make the cut, and I rearrange anything that needs it. Sometimes I put things right back where they were, but other times I move them around or try a new arrangement, just to keep things interesting. Some people rearrange the furniture; I rearrange my yarn. And anyway, yarn is made for squishing, not for collecting dust. The longer it sits untouched and out of sight, the more likely it is that critters will find their way into your yarn cubbies and set up house.

If a big annual stash reorganization day (or weekend) isn't your style, make a conscious effort to spot organize throughout the year so that every section has been emptied and sorted at least once every twelve months. Figure out what works for you, but don't assume that getting organized once will keep it organized forever. Your stash will evolve with every new skein that comes home with you, and keeping it in shape is an active process.

Guarding Against Pests

One of the biggest worries for any yarn lover is the fear of moths, mice and other yarn-loving pests. Your best defense is a good offense, and it pays to be diligent. Here are my top-five tried-and-true pest prevention strategies:

1. **Completely clean out every yarn drawer, cupboard and basket at least once a year.** I like to add a few drops of lavender essential oil to a clean, damp cloth and use it to wipe out every cubby, every surface and every container. Let the surfaces dry completely before you return the yarn. Not only will lavender refresh your space, but studies have found that lavender can work as a natural moth deterrent too.

2. **Sachets made of lavender or cedar (fresh or made with essential oils) are a safe and effective deterrent**. Keep sachets tucked throughout your stash and refresh them often. The strong scent is what deters pests, so they become less effective as the scent fades. I like to refresh my sachets with a few drops of essential oil every few months to keep them fragrant.

3. **Vacuum your space—every inch of it.** Vacuum the floors, corners and underneath your shelves. Use the vacuum hose to get around all the nooks and crannies. Carpet beetles and moths will hide out in unexpected places and will have their very own picnic on your favorite skeins if you're not careful.

4. **Act offensively.** When you bring home a new basket for yarn storage—especially one you ordered online or picked up at an outdoor market—stick it in the freezer for 72 hours (if possible) to ensure that you don't introduce any unexpected pests to your stash. My only pest issues happened to yarn that I had stored in a basket I bought at a farmers' market, so I take extra care to put baskets made of woven or braided natural fibers into the freezer for a few days before I use them to store yarn.

5. **Act defensively.** If you do notice a few bites in your yarn, you'll need to act fast to prevent further damage. Bag up all your yarn in plastic trash bags and close them tightly. Depending on how much freezer space you have, place each bag in the freezer for 72 hours before returning the skeins to your stash. (This is easier to do if you have a chest freezer with extra room in it, but do the best you can.) This process can help kill off moth larvae and prevent them from doing more damage to the yarn in your stash.

Keeping your yarn organized is only half the battle. The other half is keeping it safe. Store your yarn in a cool, dry place, out of direct sunlight. Keep it away from doors and windows that lead directly outside, as some critters will ride in on the hems of jackets, pants and shoes. Whatever you do, don't bag it all up and store it away in the dark. Having yarn out in the open may seem counterintuitive to keeping it safe from moths and other critters, but fresh air and regular squishing can keep your stash from becoming a cozy nest for an uninvited guest. The less access you have to your stash, the more inviting it is for critters looking for a new home base.

Creative Shifts and Troubleshooting

What works for you today may not work for you in a few years, so it's important to revisit your system periodically and make sure it's still the best use of your space and resources. As your interests, skills and hobbies change, you may find that some of what's in your stash doesn't belong there anymore. Part of your annual stash reboot is checking in with yourself to see if having two cubbies full of self-striping sock yarn still makes sense for the knitter you are today. Are you still knitting with boucle, or have you decided it's not for you? Reevaluate your space so you can be sure you're making the best use of it.

Red Flags

The only way to really know if your system is working is to use it. It's not meant to be so precious that you're worried about messing it up. If it gets messy again quickly or is hard to keep organized, consider it a challenge and shake things up a bit to see if you can find the source of the problem. If it's not easy to maintain, that's a sign that you haven't landed on the right system yet.

Here are a few red flags and how to troubleshoot them:

1. Are new yarn purchases still in the bags and/ or piled on top of other surfaces because you haven't had time to put them away yet? An ideal stash makes it quick and easy to put away your latest purchase. If it takes more than a few seconds to put new skeins where they belong, you might want to consider a few adjustments to the way you're sorting or storing your yarn.

2. Are you able to find what you're looking for in less than a minute or two? If not, is it possible that there are too many barriers between you and the skeins you want to use? Are there too many layers or stacks of items to dig through? It's one thing if you're just browsing your stash and trying to decide what you want to use, but if you're looking for specific yarn that you know you have on hand, then you should be able to put your hands on it in less than 2 minutes because you've already organized your stash and you have a system that makes it easy to know where to find things. A good system is easy to use and easy to maintain.

3. How long does it take to visually assess what you have? If you're preparing for a trip to the yarn store, can you set eyes on what you have relatively quickly so you can look for gaps? I may not always have a chance to count actual skeins or make a list before I go yarn shopping,

but since I have eyes on my stash on a regular basis, I know pretty well what I have and what I need. Shopping is so much easier when you eliminate most of the guesswork.

4. Do you find yourself accidentally bringing home yarn that's just like what you already have? This can be a sign that you're not putting eyes on your stash often enough to keep a mental picture of what you have and what you need. If you can't change your system and if storing your stash in a visible way isn't an option, then be sure to keep a written record of what you have so you can scan your spreadsheet instead. The longer it takes to figure out what you want to shop for, the more likely you are to waste resources on things you don't need or won't end up using.

5. How easy is it for you to spot organize sections of your stash when you have a few extra minutes? Keeping your stash in bite-sized portions makes it easier to manage, search and use. If it's necessary to overhaul your entire stash every time you want to tidy things up, then you may not have your stash broken into small enough sections to make it user-friendly.

6. Do you have to dig to get to the yarn you want? This goes along with keeping yarn in smaller segments, but if you find yourself having to physically dig to get to what you need, your system isn't going to work for the long term. Digging through large piles of yarn makes it hard to keep things in order, and it results in many like-skeins being separated from each other. (It's also a very good way to end up with a mangled mess of yarn barf.)

You are a fiber artist, and the yarn in your stash is your medium. You deserve to feel joyful and abundant when you use it. Make your stash a place that inspires you by curating it so that it's perfect for the maker you are today. And as your creative journey evolves, let your stash evolve with you so that you are always ready for the next cast-on.

Knitting with Your Stash (plus 10 Stash-Busting Patterns!)

A well-curated stash will offer you the flexibility to make almost any project you like, regardless of how much yarn it calls for. But there will always be leftovers and odd skeins that find their way into your stash that need to be put to good use. In this section, I want to help you see the potential in yarn you might otherwise bypass because it's a smaller quantity than you need, is the wrong weight for your project or doesn't seem like it will work with other skeins in your stash.

Like I said at the start, stash yarn is just yarn you already own. So really, any project can be a stash project . . . it just depends on what you have. The projects in this book are meant to be more than just patterns; they're tools to show you a different way to work with stash yarn. It's one thing to buy the same yarn and same colors that a pattern recommends, but it's something very different to choose yarn and colors based on your existing inventory. Sometimes it takes a little creativity and detective work to get it right. We'll take some of the guesswork out of the process in this section.

Making yarn substitutions is a way of life for most of us. Sometimes the recommended yarn is no longer available, and other times it might not be in your budget. When making a yarn substitution using your stash, there are four things you absolutely must keep in mind:

1. **Fiber content will affect your results.** Consider the reasons a pattern might call for a specific kind of fiber, and be prepared for your results to change if you use something different. For example, a pattern designed for superwash yarn may be relying on the drape of the fiber to achieve the right results. Likewise, a pattern designed for rugged cables may droop and sag if it's knit with a bamboo fiber instead of rustic wool. Ideally, if you can substitute yarn with the same or similar kind of fiber content than the pattern suggestions (wool, cotton, etc.) your results will be more reliable.

2. **When it comes time to block your project, superwash yarn will grow a lot more than traditional (non-superwash) yarn.** If the pattern is written for superwash yarn, then the instructions will take that growth into account, and vice versa if it's written for traditional yarn. If you are making a substitution, you'll need to adapt accordingly, knowing that yours may grow more or less than the pattern anticipates. (This also applies to certain kinds of fiber— some grow far more than others.)

3. **Gauge is critical.** Gauge is so incredibly important, even if you're not making yarn substitutions. Gauge is what makes garments fit. It contributes to how much yarn you use. And it is foundational to the fabric you create for your project. Even slight variations in gauge can make a huge difference. The only way to know if the yarn you want to use will be a good substitute is to knit a proper gauge swatch and measure it. Ideally, the swatch should be 5 x 5 inches (13 x 13 cm) so you can measure over 4 inches (10 cm) away from the edges. Always wet block your swatch, pat it dry with a towel and pin it flat (taut) to a blocking mat until it dries. Unpin it and let it rest for a few minutes before you measure. If you don't get gauge—or if your gauge is close—adjust your needle size and swatch again.

4. **Read the yarn label.** Various yarns in the same weight category (fingering, sport, worsted, etc.) are not necessarily the exact same weight. There are heavier and lighter yarns in every category, and those differences can affect your gauge and the overall fit of your project. Look at the yarn specifics in the pattern: the yardage, the weight and the fiber content. Compare those stats to the yarn you want to use from your stash. The closer you can get to the same yardage per weight and same or similar fiber content, the more consistent your results will be. This doesn't mean that you can't make wildly different substitutions, but you'll need to be realistic about how much your chosen yarn might affect your project. The more you experiment with fiber substitutions and figure out what works, the more successful your efforts will be. It's just knitting, and every project is good practice for the next one.

Working with the Color Wheel

In this pattern section, we'll use the color wheel to demonstrate how to create interesting color pairings from your stash. The color wheel can eliminate guesswork and make it easier to produce eye-catching combos you might never have considered. I've broken down three of my favorite ways to use the color wheel and provided a pattern for each one so you can put it into practice with your stash. In some cases, you can even mix multiple yarn weights in the same project! (See the Color Theory Shawl on page 89.)

A word to the wise: When it comes to working with limited quantities, you may run out of yarn before you run out of pattern. If that happens, don't panic. The Color Theory Socks (page 81) are a great example of what to do if the yarn runs out and you have to improvise. In keeping with the theme of the book, I used yarn from my stash for every project, and these socks gave me the opportunity to show you how to pivot when the yarn runs out right at the very end. I added a couple of extra stripes and kept going. You can too.

Color Theory Socks

If you love color, but don't always know how to wear it, these socks are the perfect gateway. Search your stash for smaller quantities of beautiful yarn that deserve center stage, and don't be afraid to go bold. Classic stripes are an ideal canvas for experimentation, and a little bit goes a long way in this small project. You can show off your socks if you want to, or you can keep your brave color choice a secret between you and your shoes.

Even those who love color and wear it often may find it challenging to create winning combinations in their projects. Working with a color wheel makes it easy to create expert pairings that look like they were meant for each other, and these socks are the perfect small project to experiment and see how well you like your colors together.

Sock Yarn Tip: *Handknit socks will last significantly longer if you use wool that's been reinforced with nylon or silk. Look for yarn that has a nice, tight twist (often called a high-energy twist), and avoid single ply yarns, which will leave you with holey socks in a matter of days.*

Here's how to use the color wheel to choose your yarn for this project:

1. Choose a fingering weight skein from your stash as your main color. Ideally, you'll want a solid, tonal or semisolid color for best results.

2. Find your main color on the color wheel (or something close to it), and then check the wheel to identify the color directly opposite from it. This is the complementary color. In my case, I've selected an orange for my main color and a shade of blue for my contrast. This contrast yarn can be a mini (25 to 30 grams) or a partial skein.

3. Choose a neutral for your second contrast color. You won't need much, so minis or leftovers will work nicely. My neutral is a simple cream color, which creates a lovely spacer between the other colors I chose for my project. When in doubt, I recommend either white, cream, gray, black, brown or navy for your neutral. The more contrast between the neutral and your two colors, the better.

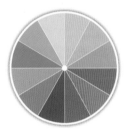

Skill Level
Intermediate

Construction
These socks are knit in the round from the cuff to the toe in one piece. The heel flap and heel turn are worked flat, and then the sock continues in the round down to the toe.

Sizes
Unisex Sizes 1 (2, 3, 4, 5, 6, 7)

To fit ankle circumference 8.5 (9.5, 10, 10.5, 10.75, 11.5, 11.75) inches / 21.5 (24, 25.5, 26.5, 27.5, 29, 30) cm

Size advice: Socks fit best with a bit of negative ease, so measure your ankle circumference and choose the size that is 1 inch (2.5 cm) smaller than your actual ankle measurement.

Abbreviations

[ ]	brackets indicate a repeat
bet	between
BOR	beginning of row/rnd
CC	contrast color (CC1, CC2, etc.)
dec	decrease(s)(d)
DPNs	double-pointed needles
k	knit
k2tog	knit two st together (dec 1)
kfb	knit into the front and back of next st
MC	main color
p	purl
p2tog	purl two st together (dec 1)
rep	repeat
rnd	round
RS	right side
ssk	slip, slip, k2tog (dec 1)
st	stitch/stitches
swyib	slip 1 st purlwise with working yarn held in back
WS	wrong side

Materials	
Yarn	Fingering weight, superwash merino wool/nylon blend, 420–450 yards (384–411 m) per 100-g skein **MC:** 400 yards (366 m) (orange) **CC1:** Complementary color: 35–50 yards (32–46 m) (blue) **CC2:** Neutral: 35–50 yards (32–46 m) (white/cream)
Needles	**For cuff:** US 1 (2.25 mm) DPNs **For body:** US 2 (2.75 mm) (or size needed to obtain gauge) DPNs
Gauge	34 st x 46 rnds = 4 inches (10 cm) with largest needle in stockinette stitch in the rnd, after blocking
Notions	Darning needle to weave in ends Waste yarn for holding stitches **Optional:** Crochet hook (size B or C) if using Russian grafting method to close the top of your socks Blocking mat and pins

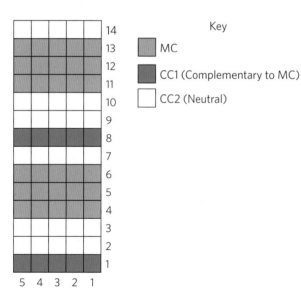

Key

■ MC

■ CC1 (Complementary to MC)

□ CC2 (Neutral)

Color Theory Socks Pattern

With US 1 (2.25 mm) DPNs and MC, cast on 64 (72, 76, 80, 84, 88, 92) st using the Estonian cast-on method (this method creates a stretchy top ridge for your sock cuff).

Row 1 (RS): [K2, p2] rep bet brackets to end. Divide st onto three DPNs and join to work in the rnd.

Rnd 2: [K2, p2] rep bet brackets to end of rnd.

Rep rnd 2 until ribbing measures 2 inches (5 cm) from cast-on edge.

On the next rnd, transition to US 2 (2.75 mm) DPNs.

Next Rnd: With MC, k to end of rnd.

Join CC1 and begin color chart, working in stockinette stitch (knitting every rnd), and repeating the chart rnds 1–14 in order until ankle measures 6 inches (15 cm) from cast-on edge. Cut MC and CC2 before you proceed.

Reinforced Heel Flap (worked flat)—worked with CC1

Heel Setup: Starting at the BOR, slip the first 32 (36, 38, 40, 42, 44, 46) st to waste yarn (this will be the instep/top of foot)—you will work back and forth on the remaining st for the heel flap, flat. Your yarn should be in position to work a WS row first. With CC1, purl this first row, then continue to Setup Rows as follows (see below Note):

> **Note:** As you proceed, do not slip the first st of every row on the heel flap—it will interfere with your ability to pick up st along the heel gusset. Work the first st of every row nice and tight to keep a tidy edge and ensure a secure gusset. You will be instructed to slip the first st later when turning the heel but be sure not to do it unless indicated. This is a traditional, reinforced heel known as a Dutch Heel, or a variation of a Square Heel.

Setup Row 1 (dec) (RS): K2tog, [swyib, k1] rep bet brackets to end of row—1 st dec.

Setup Row 2 (WS): P to end of row.

Heel Row 1 (RS): K1, [swyib, k1] rep bet brackets to end of row.

Heel Row 2 (WS): P to end of row.

Work these two rows a total of 14 (16, 18, 20, 22, 24, 26) times.

> **Note:** The slipped st will be more pronounced, and there will be half as many slipped st as you have actual rows. If you lose track of your rows, simply count a column of st on the heel flap. When you have 15 (17, 19, 21, 23, 25, 27) st in the column (the setup rows and the total repeats), it's time to turn the heel. You will maintain the [swyib, k1] pattern that you've established as you work the heel flap, so be sure to keep the slipped st aligned in the same columns as established.

Heel Turn Row 1 (RS): Work across heel flap in pattern to last 10 (12, 12, 12, 14, 14, 14) st. Stop and turn.

Heel Turn Row 2 (WS): Slip the first st (purlwise), then p to last 10 (12, 12, 12, 14, 14, 14) st. Stop and turn.

Heel Turn Row 3 (dec) (RS): Slip the first st (purlwise), then work in pattern to last 11 (13, 13, 13, 15, 15, 15) st. Work the next two st together using the ssk decrease (this decrease will consist of the st before and after the gap from where you stopped and turned on the last row). Stop and turn. This decrease will close the gap—1 st dec.

Heel Turn Row 4 (dec) (WS): Slip the first st (purlwise), then p to last 11 (13, 13, 13, 15, 15, 15) st. Work the next two st together using the p2tog decrease (this decrease will consist of the st before and after the gap from where you stopped and turned on the last row). Stop and turn. This decrease will close the gap—1 st dec.

Heel Turn Row 5 (dec) (RS): Slip the first st (purlwise), then work in pattern to the gap, ssk (closing the gap), stop and turn—1 st dec.

Heel Turn Row 6 (dec) (WS): Slip the first st (as if to purl), then purl across to gap, p2tog (closing the gap), stop and turn—1 st dec.

Rep Heel Turn Rows 5 and 6, working in pattern to the st before the gap, then working a ssk to close the gap on the RS and a p2tog to close the gap on the WS (decreasing 1 st each row). You should have one st fewer left at the end of the row each time. Continue this process until all heel st have been worked (turned) and there are no more st left at the end of the row on the RS or WS. You should end after a WS row, ready to work a RS row—11 (11, 13, 15, 13, 15, 17) st remain.

Next Row (inc) (RS): Using the next color in your stripe sequence (based on where you left off before working the heel flap), kfb into the first st (to return to an even number of st), then k across the heel flap. Do not turn. Use another DPN to divide the heel flap st equally (or almost equally) in two. You should have the heel st evenly (or nearly) divided onto two needles. Starting at the center of the heel with the second needle, and beginning just after the st you've already worked on that needle, use the tip of the needle to pick up and k 14 (16, 18, 20, 22, 24, 26) st along the edge of the gusset.

Place the instep st back onto a DPN needle and work the instep in established stripe pattern across the top of the foot.

Use the other needle holding half of the heel st to pick up and k 14 (16, 18, 20, 22, 24, 26) st along the edge of the gusset on the other side of the sock (if it is easier to do this with an extra needle, you can do that and then transfer the st to the needle holding the half of the heel st)—72 (80, 88, 96, 100, 108, 116) st.

Continue working the gusset shaping and foot in the rnd as follows. Your BOR should be at the center of the heel (you will see that this is where the working yarn is sitting in the bottom left photo).

Going forward, we will refer to the needles as shown in the photo.

GUSSET REPEAT RNDS

Rnd 1 (dec): Starting at BOR (and using the next color in stripe sequence), k to last 2 st on Needle #1, k2tog. K across Needle #2. At the beginning of Needle #3, ssk, k to end— 2 sts dec.

Rnd 2 (dec): K across Needle #1, k across Needle #2, k across Needle #3 to end.

Rep these two rnds until you have 64 (72, 76, 80, 84, 88, 92) st.

Gusset Shaping is now complete.

FOOT

Continue knitting the foot in the rnd in stockinette stitch (knitting every rnd), maintaining the stripe sequence as established until foot measures 2 (2, 2.5, 2.5, 2.75, 2.75, 3) inches / 5 (5, 6, 6, 7, 7, 7.5) cm shorter than the length of your foot.

TOE SHAPING

Cut MC and CC2 and continue the toe shaping with CC1.

> **Note:** *If you run low on CC1, transition to MC and/or CC2 to finish the remainder of the toe, as shown in the example.*

Rnd 1 (dec): With CC1, and starting with Needle #1, k to 4 st before the end of Needle #1, ssk, k2. Beginning on Needle #2, k2, k2tog, k to last 4 st on Needle #2, ssk, k2. Beginning on Needle #3, k2, k2tog, k to end—4 sts dec.

Rnd 2: With CC1, k to end of rnd.

Rep these two rnds until 32 (36, 40, 40, 44, 44, 48) st remain.

Continue toe shaping by decreasing every rnd as follows:

Next Rnds (dec): With CC1, and starting with Needle #1, k to 4 st before the end of Needle #1, ssk, k2. Beginning on Needle #2, k2, k2tog, k to last 4 st on Needle #2, ssk, k2. Beginning on Needle #3, k2, k2tog, k to end of rnd—4 sts dec.

Continue decreasing every rnd until 12 (12, 12, 12, 16, 16, 16) st remain. Divide the st evenly onto two needles (top and bottom) and then close the toe using either Kitchener st or Russian grafting.

Weave in ends on the WS. Wet block. Soak in lukewarm water with a splash of fiber wash for 20 minutes to gently cleanse and relax the fiber. Press out excess water and lay flat to dry, pinning gently along the top edge and heel. Turn as needed for even drying.

Repeat these instructions for second sock.

FINISHED ANKLE AND FOOT CIRCUMFERENCE

7.5 (8.5, 9, 9.5, 10, 10.5, 10.75) inches / 19 (21.5, 23, 24, 25.5, 26.5, 27.5) cm

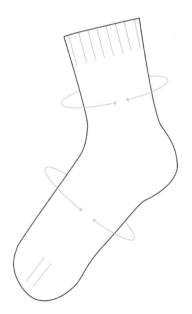

Color Theory Cowl

One of the benefits of keeping a home yarn stash is having the opportunity to mix and match colors you might not normally use together. The color theory projects in this book were designed to make you feel like a pro when matching colors, and in this design, we're using an analogous color palette, which means using three colors that are next to each other on the wheel. I chose to work with an orange/red combination for mine, but you can choose any three colors that sit next to each other on the wheel.

Don't be afraid to use a skein of variegated yarn as one of your three main colors, as long as it fits the analogous color profile. The addition of one neutral "pop" color (white, cream, black, brown, gray or beige) helps create balance and intention in the stripe sequence. My neutral is a cream because I like the high contrast, but use whatever you like to create the look you want.

Stockinette is a friend to ANY yarn, which makes this pattern an excellent stash-buster. You can use absolutely anything you have on hand: speckles, tweed, variegated, handspun, sparkles, you name it. If you're a member of a hand-dyed yarn club or tend to buy souvenir skeins when you visit new places, you will love this project for using special skeins that may otherwise be sitting in your stash too long.

Choose your three analogous colors plus one neutral, and test your theories in a swatch to make sure you like them together before you dive in. If something doesn't feel quite right with your combination, try a different shade of one of the same colors to see if it's a better fit.

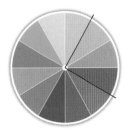

Skill Level
Advanced Beginner

Construction
This project is knit in the round as a striped tube, then twisted once to create a Möbius loop. The live stitches on each end are grafted together to create a closed loop for a wearable cowl that sits nicely around the neck.

Sizes
One size (finished measurements will vary based on your yarn choice but will be 12 inches [30 cm] in height). Circumference depends on yardage, but should be no less than 24 inches (61 cm) circumference when finished and grafted but may be significantly longer depending on how long you want to make it and how much yarn you have.

Abbreviations

C1	Color 1 (darkest color)
C2	Color 2 (medium shade)
C3	Color 3 (lightest shade)
C4	Neutral
k	knit
pm	place marker
rnd	round
RS	right side
st	stitch/stitches
WS	wrong side

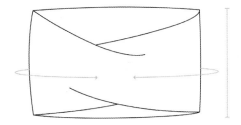

Materials	
Yarn	Fingering weight, 430–460 yards (393–421 m) per 100-g skein **C1:** Analogous color 1 (red) **C2:** Analogous color 2 (variegated dark orange) **C3:** Analogous color 3 (orange) **C4:** Neutral (cream)
Yarn Note	This project works best with four full skeins of yarn with approximately the same yardage each.
Needles	US 4 (3.5 mm) (or size needed to obtain gauge) 24-inch (61-cm) circular needle
Gauge	26 st x 32 rnds = 4 inches (10 cm) in stockinette stitch in the round, after blocking (row gauge is not critical)
Notions	Waste yarn for provisional cast-on Stitch marker Darning needle to weave in ends Spare needle (same size or smaller than used for your project) for grafting Blocking mats and pins

Color swatching: Knit a striped swatch with all four colors represented, and wet block your swatch, laying it flat to dry, to test for colorfastness. If your colors are not safe together, you may still proceed, but just steam block the finished cowl rather than wet block it.

Color Theory Cowl Pattern

With US 4 (3.5 mm) 24-inch (61-cm) circular needle and waste yarn, cast on 156 st* using a provisional cast-on method. Do not join in the rnd yet.

*This cast-on can easily be made larger or smaller to accommodate the amount of yarn you have. If you have less than full skeins, consider casting on 136 stitches instead—it will make the cowl tube a little narrower but still perfectly wearable.

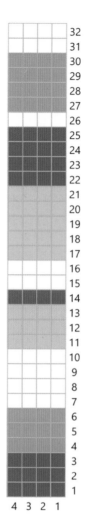

Key

- ☐ Neutral
- ■ Color 1
- ■ Color 2
- ■ Color 3

Chart Note: *The chart colors are approximate to make them easier to differentiate. For best results, assign your colors in order from darkest to lightest (darkest being Color 1, and lightest being Color 3), and select a contrasting neutral for balance. My sample shows a variegated yarn for Color 2. I recommend no more than one variegated yarn in this project for best results, but feel free to experiment.*

Next Row (RS): With C1, k to end of row, then pm and join to work in the rnd. You will count this as chart row 1.

Beginning with the next rnd (rnd 2) on the chart, work the stripe pattern rnds 1–32 in order, working in the rnd and working in stockinette stitch (knitting every rnd). Rep the chart rnds 1–32 in order until you have consumed nearly all your yarn. You should have a long, striped tube—do not bind off.

GRAFTING

Weave in ends on WS. Make one twist in your cowl to create a Möbius loop. Remove the waste yarn from the provisional cast-on and place these st onto a second needle. Graft both ends of live st together on the RS using Kitchener st or Russian grafting. Thread remaining end into the inside of tube.

Steam block (if there is a risk of colors bleeding) or wet block as follows: Soak in lukewarm water with a splash of fiber wash for 20 minutes to gently cleanse and relax the fiber. Press out excess water and lay flat to dry. Turn as needed for even drying.

Color Theory Shawl

If playing with color is your jam, and you aren't afraid to experiment with different weights of yarn in the same project, you'll love the possibilities with this shawl. This is one of the simplest projects you'll ever knit. (You don't have to count stitches or even worry about matching yarn weights or gauge.)

This pattern uses a triad color combination, which means using three equidistant colors on the wheel. As you've probably noticed, I nearly always like to include a neutral shade for balance. I've chosen the three colors marked on the wheel for mine, but you can move anywhere around the wheel and try

different combinations that work for what you have in your stash. For this trio to work, be sure they're the same distance apart all the way around the wheel. Keep in mind that your yarn doesn't have to match the color wheel exactly. This is just a starting point.

Because this pattern is flexible enough to mix and match yarn weights, you might knit a swatch with your chosen yarns to see how they work together and to test your color choices. Some fibers will work better than others in this capacity, so experimentation is key.

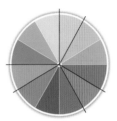

Skill Level
Advanced Beginner

Construction
Worked from the center neck out in a crescent shape with increases on both the right side and wrong side rows (at the edges), your shawl will grow quickly in width without adding bulk to the body. You can carry the colors up the side throughout most of the project, but you may prefer to cut colors between the longer stretches.

Size
One size (finished measurements will vary based on your yarn choices)

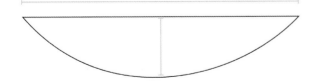

Abbreviations

[ ]	brackets indicate a repeat
bet	between
BO	bind off
CC	contrast color (CC1, CC2, etc.)
CO	cast on
inc	increase/increases
k	knit
ktbl	knit through the back loop (this will close up the yo from the previous row)
k-yo-k	knit, yarn over, then knit again into the same stitch (2 st inc)
MC	main color
p	purl
rep	repeat
rnd	round
RS	right side
st	stitch/stitches
WS	wrong side
yo	yarn over (inc 1)

Materials	
Yarn	4 skeins of 100 grams each of any mix of yarn weights as long as you have a minimum of 220 yards (201 m) per skein
	MC: Neutral (cream or any solid color)
	CC1: Triad color 1 (hot pink)
	CC2: Triad color 2 (blue)
	CC3: Triad color 3 (gold)
Needles	US 6 (4 mm)* 32-inch (81-cm) circular needle for mostly fingering or sport weights
	or
	US 7 (4.5 mm)* 32-inch (81-cm) circular needle for mostly worsted/DK yarn weights
	*Adjust your needle size as necessary to create the fabric you prefer for your shawl.
Gauge	Because of the variation of yarn weights in this project, gauge will vary.
Notions	Darning needle to weave in ends
	Blocking mats and pins

Color swatching: I recommend knitting a striped swatch and wet blocking it so you can test colorfastness before you begin your project.

Color Theory Shawl Pattern

With appropriate 32-inch (81-cm) circular needle size for your chosen yarn (I used a US 7 [4.5 mm] for my version, worked in a combination of DK and heavy fingering weight yarn) and MC, cast on 3 st using knitted cast-on method.

SETUP
Row 1 (RS): [K-yo-k] rep bet brackets 3 times—9 st.

Row 2 (WS): P1, yo, p to last st, yo, p1—11 st.

Rows 3, 5, 7, 9 (RS): K1, ktbl, k-yo-k, k to last 3 st, k-yo-k, ktbl, k1—4 st inc.

Row 4, 6, 8, 10 (WS): P1, yo, p to last st, yo, p1—2 st inc.

STITCH COUNT CHECK-IN
35 st

SECTION ONE
Row 1 (RS): With CC1, k1, ktbl, k-yo-k, k to last 3 st, k-yo-k, ktbl, k1—4 st inc.

Row 2 (WS): With CC1, k1, yo, k to last st, yo, k1—2 st inc.

Row 3 (RS): With MC, k1, ktbl, k-yo-k, k to last 3 st, k-yo-k, ktbl, k1—4 st inc.

Row 4 (WS): With MC, p1, yo, p to last st, yo, p1—2 st inc.

Row 5 (RS): With CC2, k1, ktbl, k-yo-k, k to last 3 st, k-yo-k, ktbl, k1—4 st inc.

Row 6 (WS): With CC2, k1, yo, k to last st, yo, k1—2 st inc.

Row 7 (RS): With MC, k1, ktbl, k-yo-k, k to last 3 st, k-yo-k, ktbl, k1—4 st inc.

Row 8 (WS): With MC, p1, yo, p to last st, yo, p1—2 st inc.

Row 9 (RS): With CC3, k1, ktbl, k-yo-k, k to last 3 st, k-yo-k, ktbl, k1—4 st inc.

Row 10 (WS): With CC3, k1, yo, k to last st, yo, k1—2 st inc.

Row 11 (RS): With MC, k1, ktbl, k-yo-k, k to last 3 st, k-yo-k, ktbl, k1—4 st inc.

Row 12 (WS): With MC, p1, yo, p to last st, yo, p1—2 st inc.

Rep rows 1–12 twice more (for a total of three repeats) to complete Section One, then continue to Section Two.

Don't worry about st counts—it won't hinder the design if you miss an increase here or there. Please note that every time you repeat Section One, you will work rows 1–12 three times for the full Section One to be completed before moving on to Section Two.

SECTION TWO

Row 1 (RS): With CC1, k1, ktbl, k-yo-k, k to last 3 st, k-yo-k, ktbl, k1—4 st inc.

Row 2 (WS): With CC1, k1, yo, k to last st, yo, k1—2 st inc.

Row 3 (RS): With CC1, k1, ktbl, k-yo-k, k to last 3 st, k-yo-k, ktbl, k1—4 st inc.

Row 4 (WS): With CC1, p1, yo, p to last st, yo, p1—2 st inc.

Row 5 (RS): With CC1, k1, ktbl, k-yo-k, k to last 3 st, k-yo-k, ktbl, k1—4 st inc.

Row 6 (WS): With CC1, k1, yo, k to last st, yo, k1—2 st inc.

Row 7 (RS): With MC, k1, ktbl, k-yo-k, k to last 3 st, k-yo-k, ktbl, k1—4 st inc.

Row 8 (WS): With MC, p1, yo, p to last st, yo, p1—2 st inc.

COLOR TRANSITION

Row 9 (RS): With CC2, k1, ktbl, k-yo-k, k to last 3 st, k-yo-k, ktbl, k1—4 st inc.

Row 10 (WS): With CC2, k1, yo, k to last st, yo, k1—2 st inc.

Row 11 (RS): With CC2, k1, ktbl, k-yo-k, k to last 3 st, k-yo-k, ktbl, k1—4 st inc.

Row 12 (WS): With CC2, p1, yo, p to last st, yo, p1—2 st inc.

Row 13 (RS): With CC2, k1, ktbl, k-yo-k, k to last 3 st, k-yo-k, ktbl, k1—4 st inc.

Row 14 (WS): With CC2, k1, yo, k to last st, yo, k1—2 st inc.

Row 15 (RS): With MC, k1, ktbl, k-yo-k, k to last 3 st, k-yo-k, ktbl, k1—4 st inc.

Row 16 (WS): With MC, p1, yo, p to last st, yo, p1—2 st inc.

COLOR TRANSITION

Row 17 (RS): With CC3, k1, ktbl, k-yo-k, k to last 3 st, k-yo-k, ktbl, k1—4 st inc.

Row 18 (WS): With CC3, k1, yo, k to last st, yo, k1—2 st inc.

Row 19 (RS): With CC3, k1, ktbl, k-yo-k, k to last 3 st, k-yo-k, ktbl, k1—4 st inc.

Row 20 (WS): With CC3, p1, yo, p to last st, yo, p1—2 st inc.

Row 21 (RS): With CC3, k1, ktbl, k-yo-k, k to last 3 st, k-yo-k, ktbl, k1—4 st inc.

Row 22 (WS): With CC3, k1, yo, k to last st, yo, k1—2 st inc.

Row 23 (RS): With MC, k1, ktbl, k-yo-k, k to last 3 st, k-yo-k, ktbl, k1—4 st inc.

Row 24 (WS): With MC, p1, yo, p to last st, yo, p1—2 st inc.

END OF SECTION TWO

Rep Sections One and Two, including both Color Transitions, in order until you are nearly out of the MC, with enough left to complete a WS row (if possible). Work the final WS row before you continue. Consider the look of your shawl when determining where to stop, and don't be afraid to add a few rows of a final color to balance your stripe sequence.

CONCLUSION

With any one of the three contrast colors from your project (ideally the next color in the sequence, but any color from your project is fine), work a picot bind-off at the start of the next RS row as follows:

Step 1: CO 2 st using knitted cast-on method.

Step 2: BO 4 st.

Step 3: Slip the remaining st from your right needle back to your left needle.

Rep steps 1–3 until all st have been bound off on your project.

Weave in ends on the WS. Wet block, soaking in a luke-warm basin of clean water with a splash of fiber wash for at least 20 minutes, or until the fiber is fully satura-ted. Drain and press out excess water, then lay flat. Pin, starting at the top center neck of your shawl (where you cast on); pin the top edge straight across horizontally on your blocking mats. From there, draw out the crescent shape starting in the center and pulling the shawl edges downward to expand the crescent shape and draw the fabric taut. Pin flat to enhance the shape and let dry completely.

Making Leftovers Look Intentional

Just because you might happen to be using smaller or limited quantities of yarn doesn't mean you can't make them look fabulous. When working with leftover yarn, look for patterns that use contrast color with intention. The more sections of color a pattern has, the more opportunities you have to experiment.

When in doubt, borrow some of the color wheel techniques from Working with the Color Wheel (page 79), and use them to help you come up with ideas for the projects in this section. The Block Party patterns feature the same simple colorwork details, but offer you three different canvases to experiment. If you're not entirely sure about your color choices, try them first in the Block Party Beanie (page 97) before you commit to Block Party Pullover for Kids (page 101) and Block Party Pullover for Grown Ups (page 107).

Patterns like these will remind you of why it's important to keep neutrals and solid skeins in your stash. They can help you stretch what you have and will make it easier to use trophy skeins that might otherwise spend too much time sitting on a shelf.

Block Party Beanie

Color blocking is one of my favorite ways to use stash yarn, especially when working with smaller quantities and leftovers. The design details are so tidy that you can implement a range of colors (even variegated or speckled yarns) for a gorgeous, gift-worthy knit that looks 100 percent intentional and 0 percent scrappy.

Skill Level

Intermediate

Construction

This pattern is knit in the round from the brim to the crown. It features a ribbed brim with graphic colorwork details on the body of the design.

Sizes

Baby (Toddler, Child, Adult Medium, Adult Large)

To fit head size 15 (17, 19.25, 21.25, 23.5) inches / 38 (43, 49, 54, 59.5) cm with slight negative ease at the brim for a good fit

See Finished Measurements on page 99.

Abbreviations

[ ]	brackets indicate a repeat
bet	between
CC	contrast color
dec	decrease(s)(d)
DPNs	double-pointed needles
inc	increase/increases
k	knit
k2tog	knit 2 st together (dec 1)
kfb	knit into front and back of same st (inc 1)
MC	main color
p	purl
pm	place marker
rep	repeat
rnd	round
RS	right side
st	stitch/stitches
WS	wrong side

Materials	
Yarn	Fingering weight, 100% wool or similar, 400 yards (366 m) per 100-g skein **MC:** 400 yards (366 m) **CC:** 160 yards (146 m)
Yarn note	**Note:** To estimate yardage for multiple contrast colors (if you'd rather use more than one), divide the contrast color yardage evenly by the number of colors you'd like to use.
Needles	**For ribbing:** US 2 (2.75 mm) 16-inch (40-cm) circular needle **For body:** US 3 (3.25 mm) (or size needed to obtain gauge) 16-inch (40-cm) circular needle **For crown decreases:** US 3 (3.25 mm) DPNs
Gauge	30 st x 36 rnds = 4 inches (10 cm) with largest needle in stockinette stitch in the rnd, after blocking
Notions	Stitch marker Darning needle to weave in ends Blocking mats and pins

Block Party Beanie Pattern

With US 2 (2.75 mm) 16-inch (40-cm) circular needle and MC, cast on 104 (120, 132, 148, 160) st using cable cast-on method. Do not join in the rnd yet. Note that the cable cast-on begins your work immediately on the RS.

Row 1 (RS): [K2, p2] rep bet bracket to end, then pm and join to work in the rnd.

Rnd 2: [K2, p2] rep bet brackets to end of rnd.

Rep rnd 2 until ribbing measures 1 (1, 1.5, 1.5, 2) inch(es) / 2.5 (2.5, 4, 4, 5) cm from cast-on edge.

On the next rnd, transition to US 3 (3.25 mm) 16-inch (40-cm) circular needle.

Next Rnd (inc): [K12 (14, 10, 11, 9), kfb], rep bet brackets 8 (8, 12, 12, 16) total times, k0 (0, 0, 4, 0)—8 (8, 12, 12, 16) sts inc.

Next 3 Rnds: K to end of rnd. Begin colorwork chart on the next rnd and work chart rnds 1–33 in order until chart has been completed.

Cut CC and continue with MC only, working in the rnd in stockinette stitch (knitting every rnd) until beanie measures 5.5 (6.5, 7.5, 8, 9) inches / 14 (16.5, 19, 20.5, 23) cm from cast-on edge. For a slouchier fit, work an additional 1 inch (2.5 cm) before starting decreases.

CROWN DECREASES

> **Note:** *Transition to DPNs as needed while you work the decrease rnds.*

Rnd 1 (dec): [K6, k2tog] rep bet brackets to end of rnd—14 (16, 18, 20, 22) st dec.

Rnd 2 (and all even rnds): Knit.

Rnd 3 (dec): [K5, k2tog] rep bet brackets to end of rnd— 14 (16, 18, 20, 22) st dec.

Rnd 5 (dec): [K4, k2tog] rep bet brackets to end of rnd— 14 (16, 18, 20, 22) st dec.

Rnd 7 (dec): [K3, k2tog] rep bet brackets to end of rnd— 14 (16, 18, 20, 22) st dec.

Rnd 9 (dec): [K2, k2tog] rep bet brackets to end of rnd— 14 (16, 18, 20, 22) st dec.

Rnd 11 (dec): [K1, k2tog] rep bet brackets to end of rnd— 14 (16, 18, 20, 22) st dec.

Rnd 13 (dec): [K2tog] rep bet brackets to end of rnd— 14 (16, 18, 20, 22) st dec.

Rnd 14 (dec): [K2tog] rep bet brackets to end of rnd—7 (8, 9, 10, 11) stitches remain.

Bind off remaining st and cut working yarn, leaving a long tail.

FINISHING

Thread the yarn tail through a darning needle and draw it through just one leg of each bound-off st on the crown. Weave in ends on the WS. Wet block. Soak in lukewarm water with a splash of fiber wash for 20 minutes to gently cleanse and relax the fiber. Press out excess water and lay flat to dry, taking care not to stretch the ribbing while it's wet. Turn as needed for even drying.

CHARTS (CHOOSE ONE)

Color codes on these charts are just a jumping-off point. Use them as a springboard for ideas as you search your stash. For a more subtle transition between blocks, consider gradients or tonals from the same color family. If you decide to use variegated colorways, be sure to alternate them with contrasting solid or semisolid colors so their details aren't lost.

Chart Note: *The design is a 2-stitch repeat, shown here over 6 stitches to make it easier to envision the full pattern.*

FINISHED MEASUREMENTS

Length (Brim to Crown): 7 (8, 9.25, 9.75, 10.75) inches / 18 (20.5, 23.5, 25, 27.5) cm

Circumference at Brim: 14 (16, 17.5, 19.75, 21.25) inches / 35.5 (40.5, 44.5, 50, 54) cm

Circumference at Body: 15 (17, 19.25, 21.25, 23.5) inches / 38 (43, 49, 54, 59.5) cm

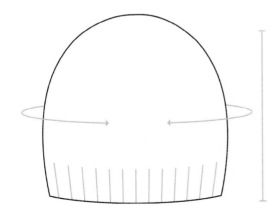

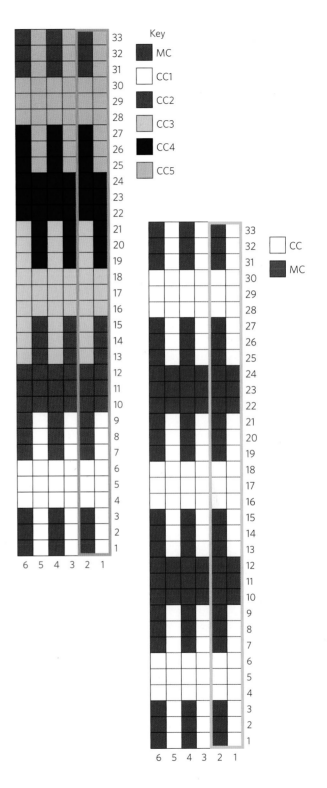

Key

■	MC
□	CC1
■	CC2
■	CC3
■	CC4
■	CC5

□	CC
■	MC

Block Party Pullover for Kids

Clever stitch details make it easy to mix and match minis or leftovers for your contrast colors to create a design that looks completely intentional. There's no need to limit yourself to a single contrast color (unless you want to). Feel free to turn every color transition into an opportunity to join a new shade.

For the ultimate stash-busting project, search your stash for leftovers and minis that may seem too small for most other purposes. Even 20 to 25 yards (18 to 23 m) of a single yarn can be useful when you use it in concert with other colors to make your project pop. If you need help mixing colors, refer to the color wheel concepts in Working with the Color Wheel (page 79). You can use the color wheel principles any time you're working with multiple colors for a project.

Skill Level
Intermediate

Construction
This top-down, circular yoke pullover is knit in one piece (no seams!) and is designed to fit newborns up to preteens.

Sizes
1 (2, 3, 4, 5, 6, 7, 8)

0–6 mo (6–12 mo, 1–2 yrs, 2–4 yrs, 4–6 yrs, 6–8 yrs, 8–10 yrs, 10–12 yrs)

This sweater is designed to fit with 2 inches (5 cm) positive ease.

See Finished Measurements on page 105.

Abbreviations

[ ]	brackets indicate a repeat
bet	between
BOR	Beginning of row/rnd
CC	contrast color
CO	cast on
dec	decrease(s)(d)
DPNs	double-pointed needles
inc	increase/increases
k	knit
k2tog	knit two st together (dec 1)
m	marker/markers
MC	main color
M1R	make one stitch, right leaning
p	purl
pm	place marker
rep	repeat
rnd	round
RS	right side
st	stitch/stitches
swyib	slip 1 st purlwise with working yarn held in back
x	indicates that size is not included in this line of instruction

Materials

Yarn	Sport weight, 100% merino and merino/Rambouillet wool or similar, 148 yards (135 m) in 50 grams **MC:** 182 (202, 208, 293, 338, 455, 475, 504) yards / 166 (185, 190, 268, 309, 416, 434, 461) m **CC:** 98 (109, 112, 158, 182, 245, 256, 271) yards / 90 (100, 102, 144, 166, 224, 234, 248) m
Needles	**For neckline:** US 4 (3.5 mm) 12- to 16-inch (30- to 40-cm) circular needle **For bottom ribbing:** US 4 (3.5 mm) 16- to 24-inch (40- to 61-cm) circular needle **For sleeve cuffs:** US 4 (3.5 mm) DPNs **For yoke and body:** US 5 (3.75 mm) (or size needed to obtain gauge) 12- to 24-inch (30- to 61-cm) circular needle (use length that is most comfortable for the size you're knitting, transition to a longer length as needed) **For sleeves:** US 5 (3.75 mm) 12-inch (30-cm) circular needle or DPNs
Gauge	22 st x 31 rnds = 4 inches (10 cm) with largest needle in stockinette stitch in the rnd, after blocking
Notions	Stitch markers Waste yarn for holding stitches Darning needle to weave in ends Blocking mats and pins

Stash-Friendly Tip: *To make use of smaller bits of stash yarns, use a different contrast color for each color transition. To estimate yardage for multiple contrast colors, divide the contrast color yardage somewhat evenly by the number of colors you'd like to use, keeping in mind that colors used at the beginning will use slightly less yardage than those used later in the yoke.*

Block Party Pullover for Kids Pattern

With US 4 (3.5 mm) 12- to 16-inch (30- to 40-cm) circular needle and using MC, cast on 76 (84, 88, 92, 92, 92, 96, 96) st using cable cast-on method. Do not join in the rnd yet. Note that the cable cast-on begins your work immediately on the RS.

Row 1 (RS): [K2, p2] rep bet brackets to end, then pm and join to work in the rnd.

Rnd 2: [K2, p2] rep bet brackets to end of rnd.

Rep rnd 2 until ribbing measures 1 (1, 1, 1, 1.5, 1.5, 1.5, 2) inch(es) / 2.5 (2.5, 2.5, 2.5, 4, 4, 4, 5) cm.

On the next rnd, transition to US 5 (3.75 mm) 12- to 24-inch (30- to 61-cm) circular needle and begin upper yoke as follows:

Next 4 Rnds (RS): K to end of rnd.

SIZES 1, 2, 3 ONLY
Next Rnd (inc): K8 (7, 9, x, x, x, x, x), [M1R, k12 (14, 14, x, x, x, x, x)] rep bet brackets to last 8 (7, 9, x, x, x, x, x) st, M1R, k to end—6 (6, 6, x, x, x, x, x) st inc.

SIZES 4, 5, 6, 7, 8 ONLY
Next Rnd (inc): Kx (x, x, 1, 7, 7, 9, 9), [M1R, kx (x, x, 5, 3, 3, 3, 3)] rep bet brackets to last x (x, x, 1, 7, 7, 9, 9) st, k to end—x (x, x, 18, 26, 26, 26, 26) st inc.

STITCH COUNT CHECK-IN
82 (90, 94, 110, 118, 118, 122, 122)

Next Rnd: Join CC and work as follows: [k1, swyib] rep bet brackets to end of rnd.

Next Rnd: With MC, [swyib, k1] rep bet brackets to end of rnd.

Next Rnd: With CC, [k1, swyib] rep bet brackets to end of rnd.

Next Rnd: With MC, [swyib, k1] rep bet brackets to end of rnd.

Next Rnd: With CC, [k1, swyib] rep bet brackets to end of rnd.

Next Rnd: With MC, [swyib, k1] rep bet brackets to end of rnd. Cut MC for now.

Next Rnd: With CC, k to end of rnd.

Next Rnd (inc): With CC, k2 (6, 2, 3, 7, 3, 7, 7), [k3 (3, 3, 4, 4, 4, 3, 3), M1R] rep bet brackets to last 2 (6, 2, 3, 7, 3, 7, 7) st, k to end—26 (26, 30, 26, 26, 28, 36, 36) st inc.

Next Rnd: With CC, k to end of rnd.

STITCH COUNT CHECK-IN

108 (116, 124, 136, 144, 146, 158, 158)

Next Rnd: With MC, [swyib, k1] rep bet brackets to end of rnd.

Next Rnd: With CC, [k1, swyib] rep bet brackets to end of rnd.

Rep these two rnds twice more (for a total of three times).

Next Rnd: With MC, k to end of rnd.

Next Rnd (inc): With MC, k2 (6, 2, 3, 7, 3, 7, 7), [k4 (4, 4, 5, 5, 5, 4, 4), M1R] rep bet brackets to last 2 (6, 2, 3, 7, 3, 7, 7) st, k to end—26 (26, 30, 26, 26, 28, 36, 36) st inc.

Next Rnd: With MC, k to end of rnd.

STITCH COUNT CHECK-IN

134 (142, 154, 162, 170, 174, 194, 194)

Next Rnd: With CC, [swyib, k1] rep bet brackets to end of rnd.

Next Rnd: With MC, [k1, swyib] rep bet brackets to end of rnd.

Rep these two rnds twice more (for a total of three times).

Next 2 Rnds: With CC, k to end of rnd.

Next Rnd (inc): k2 (6, 2, 3, 7, 3, 7, 7), [k5 (5, 5, 6, 6, 6, 5, 5), M1R] rep bet brackets to last 2 (6, 2, 3, 7, 3, 7, 7) st, k to end—26 (26, 30, 26, 26, 28, 36, 36) st inc.

STITCH COUNT CHECK-IN

160 (168, 184, 188, 196, 202, 230, 230)

Next Rnd: With MC, [swyib, k1] rep bet brackets to end of rnd.

Next Rnd: With CC, [k1, swyib] rep bet brackets to end of rnd.

Rep these two rnds twice more (for a total of three times).

Next Rnd: With MC, k to end of rnd.

Next Rnd (inc): With MC, k2 (9, 8, 4, 8, 3, 10, 3), [k6 (5, 7, 9, 9, 7, 7, 7), M1R] rep bet brackets to last 2 (9, 8, 4, 8, 3, 10, 3) st, k to end—26 (30, 24, 20, 20, 28, 30, 32) st inc.

Next Rnd: With MC, k to end of rnd.

STITCH COUNT CHECK-IN

186 (198, 208, 208, 216, 230, 260, 262)

SIZES 1, 2, 3 ONLY

With MC, k1 (5, 6, x, x, x, x, x) rnds, then move ahead to Divide for Sleeves.

SIZES 4, 5, 6, 7, 8 ONLY—CONTINUE

Next Rnd: With CC, [swyib, k1] rep bet brackets to end of rnd.

Next Rnd: With MC, [k1, swyib] rep bet brackets to end of rnd.

Rep these two rnds twice more (for a total of three times).

Next Rnd: With CC, k to end of rnd.

Next Rnd (inc): With CC, kx (x, x, 5, 8, 5, 4, 3), [kx (x, x, 11, 10, 10, 14, 8), M1R] rep bet brackets to last x (x, x, 5, 8, 5, 4, 3) st, k to end—x (x, x, 18, 20, 22, 18, 32) st inc.

Next Rnd: With CC, k to end of rnd.

STITCH COUNT CHECK-IN

x (x, x, 226, 236, 252, 278, 294)

Next Rnd: With MC, [swyib, k1] rep bet brackets to end of rnd.

Next Rnd: With CC, [k1, swyib] rep bet brackets to end of rnd.

Rep these two rnds twice more (for a total of three times). Cut CC and continue with MC only.

With MC, kx (x, x, 0, 3, 6, 8, 12) rnds then move ahead to Divide for Sleeves.

DIVIDE FOR SLEEVES

With MC, k19 (20, 21, 22, 23, 24, 27, 30) st, pm—this will be half of the right sleeve. K55 (59, 62, 69, 72, 78, 85, 87) st—this will be the sweater front. Place next 38 (40, 42, 44, 46, 48, 54, 60) st onto waste yarn—this is the left sleeve. CO 2 st under the arm, then join to the back and k next 55 (59, 62, 69, 72, 78, 85, 87) st—this is the sweater back. Place the next 38 (40, 42, 44, 46, 48, 54, 60) st onto waste yarn, removing the BOR marker—this is the right sleeve. CO 2 st under the arm, placing a new BOR marker in the center of these st. Join to the front.

You have now separated the sleeves from the body and will be working just the lower body as you proceed. You will return to work the sleeves later.

LOWER BODY STITCH COUNT

114 (122, 128, 142, 148, 160, 174, 178)

LOWER BODY

Continue knitting the lower body in the rnd, working stockinette stitch (knitting every rnd) until body measures 3 (3.5, 4, 5, 6.5, 8.5, 10.5, 11.5) inches / 7.5 (9, 10, 12.5, 16.5, 21.5, 26.5, 29) cm from the sleeve divide.

Next Rnd: With CC, [k1, swyib] rep bet brackets to end of rnd.

Next Rnd: With MC, [swyib, k1] rep bet brackets to end of rnd.

Rep these two rnds twice more (for a total of three times).

Next 2 Rnds: With CC, k to end of rnd.

Next Rnd: With MC, [swyib, k1] rep bet brackets to end of rnd.

Next Rnd: With CC, [k1, swyib] rep bet brackets to end of rnd.

Rep these two rnds twice more (for a total of three times). Cut CC and continue with MC only.

Next 3 (3, 4, 4, 5, 5, 5, 5) Rnds: With MC, k to end of rnd.

On the next rnd, transition to US 4 (3.5 mm) 16- to 24-inch (40- to 61-cm) circular needle and set up for ribbing as follows:

Rnd 1: K to end of rnd, decreasing 2 (2, 0, 2, 0, 0, 2, 2) st using k2tog, spacing your decreases evenly as you work the rnd.

LOWER RIBBING

Rnd 2: [K2, p2] rep bet brackets to end of rnd.

Rep rnd 2 until ribbing measures 1 (1, 1, 1.25, 1.5, 1.5, 1.5, 1.5) inch(es) / 2.5 (2.5, 2.5, 3, 4, 4, 4, 4) cm.

Bind off in pattern with medium tension (not too loose, not too tight). A stretchy bind-off is not necessary.

SLEEVES

With US 5 (3.75 mm) 12-inch (30-cm) circular needle or DPNs and beginning with either sleeve, retrieve the sleeve st from waste yarn and pick up the 2 st cast on under the arm. Pm at center of underarm to denote the BOR and join to knit in the rnd.

Next Rnd: K to end of rnd.

SLEEVE STITCH COUNT

40 (42, 44, 46, 48, 50, 56, 62)

Next Rnd (dec): K1, k2tog, k to 3 st before m, k2tog, k1—2 st dec.

Continue working the sleeve in the rnd in stockinette stitch (knitting every rnd), working a decrease rnd as established every 1.5 (1.25, 2, 2, 3.25, 5.5, 2.25, 2) inches / 4 (3, 5, 5, 8, 14, 5.5, 5) cm until the sleeve measures 5.5 (6.5, 7.5, 9.5, 11, 12, 13, 13.5) inches / 14 (16.5, 19, 24, 28, 30.5, 33, 34.5) cm and you have 32 (32, 36, 36, 40, 40, 44, 48) st (adjust length, as necessary, for your best fit and to account for yarn growth).

On the next rnd, transition to US 4 (3.5 mm) DPNs for the cuff and knit one rnd.

Next Rnd: [K2, p2] rep bet brackets to end of rnd.

Rep this rnd until cuff measures 1 (1, 1, 1.5, 1.5, 1.5, 1.5, 1.5) inch(es) / 2.5 (2.5, 2.5, 4, 4, 4, 4, 4) cm. Bind off in pattern with medium/loose tension.

Repeat the sleeve instructions for the second sleeve.

FINISHING

Weave in ends, including closing any gaps under the arms, as needed. Wet block. Soak in lukewarm water with a splash of fiber wash for 20 minutes to gently cleanse and relax the fiber. Press out excess water and lay flat to dry. Turn as needed for even drying.

FINISHED MEASUREMENTS

Neck circumference: 13.75 (15.25, 16, 16.75, 16.75, 16.75, 17.5, 17.5) inches / 35 (39, 40.5, 42.5, 42.5, 42.5, 44.5, 44.5) cm

Chest circumference: 20.75 (22.25, 23.25, 25.75, 27, 29, 31.5, 32.5) inches / 52.5 (56.5, 59, 65.5, 68.5, 73.5, 80, 82.5) cm

Length of lower body from underarm: 5.5 (6, 6.75, 8, 9.75, 11.75, 13.75, 14.75) inches / 14 (15, 17, 20.5, 25, 30, 35, 37.5) cm

Sleeve length: 6.5 (7.5, 8.5, 11, 12.5, 13.5, 14.5, 15) inches / 16.5 (19, 21.5, 28, 32, 34.5, 37, 38) cm

Sleeve circumference: 7.25 (7.5, 8, 8.5, 8.75, 9, 10.25, 11.25) inches / 18.5 (19, 20.5, 21.5, 22, 23, 26, 28.5) cm

Yoke depth (measured from under the ribbing to the underarm): 4 (4.5, 4.5, 5, 5.25, 5.75, 6, 6.5) inches / 10 (11.5, 11.5, 12.5, 13, 14.5, 15, 16.5) cm

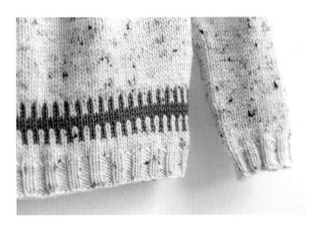

Block Party Pullover for Grown Ups

This yoke-style pullover is knit seamlessly from the top down and is a versatile way to use skeins that aren't quite enough for a sweater (at least not until you put them together). As with the other coordinating Block Party patterns in this book, you can mix and match colors you might not normally use together. Just be sure you have enough contrast between the yarns to showcase the stitch details. They can get a bit muddy if the colors are too busy or too similar.

Look for partial skeins that may be languishing in your stash. Even 45 to 50 yards (41 to 46 m) can be enough, depending on where you use them in the sweater. If you decide to use multiple colors for your contrast, use the one with the least yardage first, as the top of the yoke will consume the least amount of yarn.

Skill

Intermediate

Construction

This top-down, circular yoke pullover is knit in one piece (no seams!)

Sizes

1 (2, 3, 4, 5, 6, 7, 8, 9)

S (M, L, XL, 2XL, 3XL, 4XL, 5XL, 6XL)

Bust Circumference: 33 (37.5, 41, 45.25, 49, 53.25, 57, 61, 65) inches / 84 (95, 104, 115, 124.5, 135, 144.75, 155, 165) cm

Designed to fit with 2-inch (5-cm) positive ease.

See Finished Measurements on page 113.

Abbreviations

[ ]	brackets indicate a repeat
bet	between
BOR	beginning of row/rnd
CC	contrast color (CC1, CC2, etc.)
CO	cast on
dec	decrease(s)(d)
DPNs	double-pointed needles
inc	increase 1 st using e-loop (backward loop)
k	knit
k2tog	knit 2 stitches together (dec 1)
m	marker/markers
MC	main color
M1R	make one st, right leaning (inc 1)
p	purl
p2tog	purl two st together (dec 1)
pm	place marker
rep	repeat
rnd	round
RS	right side
st	stitch/stitches
WS	wrong side
x	indicates that size is not included in this line of instruction

Materials	
Yarn	Fingering weight, superwash merino wool/nylon blend, 420–450 yards (384–411 m) per 100-g skein **MC:** 962 (1023, 1084, 1149, 1218, 1292, 1369, 1451, 1538) yards / 880 (935, 991, 1051, 1114, 1181, 1252, 1327, 1406) m **CC1:** 218 (232, 246, 261, 276, 293, 310, 329, 349) yards / 199 (212, 225, 239, 252, 268, 283, 301, 319) m **CC2:** 196 (208, 220, 234, 248, 263, 278, 295, 313) yards / 179 (190, 201, 214, 227, 240, 254, 270, 286) m
Needles	**For neckline:** US 2 (2.75 mm) 16-inch (40-cm) circular needle **For bottom ribbing:** US 2 (2.75 mm) 24- to 40-inch (61- to 100-cm) circular needle **For sleeve cuffs:** US 2 (2.75 mm) DPNs **For yoke and body:** US 3 (3.25 mm) (or size needed to obtain gauge) 24- to 40-inch (61- to 100-cm) circular needle (use length that is most comfortable for the size you're knitting, transition to a longer length as needed) **For sleeves:** US 3 (3.25 mm) 12-inch (30-cm) circular needle or DPNs
Gauge	28 st x 36 rnds = 4 inches (10 cm) with largest needle in colorwork pattern (knit in stockinette stitch in the rnd), after blocking **Note:** Your gauge in colorwork may be tighter than in stockinette stitch, so please adjust your tension or needle size (as needed) for consistent gauge throughout the garment.

Materials	
Notions	Stitch markers Locking stitch markers Waste yarn for holding stitches Darning needle to weave in ends Blocking mat and pins

Block Party Pullover for Grown Ups Pattern

With US 2 (2.75 mm) 16-inch (40-cm) circular needle and using MC, cast on 128 (128, 128, 132, 136, 140, 140, 144, 148) st using cable cast-on method. Do not join in the rnd yet. Note that the cable cast-on begins your work immediately on the RS.

Row 1 (RS): [K2, p2] rep bet brackets to end, then pm and join to work in the rnd.

Rnd 2: [K2, p2] rep bet brackets to end of rnd.

Rep rnd 2 until ribbing measures 1.5 inches (4 cm) from cast-on edge.

On the next rnd, transition to US 3 (3.25 mm) 24- to 40-inch (61- to 100-cm) circular needle and begin upper yoke as follows:

Next Rnd (inc): K4 (4, 4, 0, 2, 4, 4, 0, 2), [k4 (3, 3, 3, 3, 3, 3, 3), M1R] rep bet brackets to last 4 (4, 4, 0, 2, 4, 4, 0, 2) st, k to end—30 (40, 40, 44, 44, 44, 48, 48) st inc.

Next Rnd: K79 (84, 84, 88, 90, 92, 92, 96, 98) st, place a side marker, k79 (84, 84, 88, 90, 92, 92, 96, 98) st to end. Stop.

> **Tip:** *If you prefer a different short row method, simply work 8 short rows in your preferred method, using the details below as a guide for the turning point. Be sure to keep your BOR and side markers in place as you create the short rows.*

Turn your work to the wrong side to begin 8 short rows using the Japanese short row method. You will need two locking markers for this technique.

Short Row 1 (WS): Slip first st to right needle (purlwise) without working it and place a locking marker on your working yarn (holding the marker to the WS of your work). P to the side marker. Stop and turn back to the RS.

Short Row 2 (RS): Slip first st to right needle (purlwise) without working it and place a locking marker on your working yarn (holding the marker to the WS of your work). K to the gap that is marked with locking marker. Using the marker to pull, draw up the marked yarn from the WS of your work and place it on the left needle as if a new st (adjusting the BOR marker, as needed, to work the short row, and then replacing it to its original location), then knit it together (k2tog) with the next st on the left needle (closing the gap) and remove locking marker. K1, stop, and turn to the wrong side.

Short Row 3 (WS): Slip first st to right needle (purlwise) without working it, place a locking marker on the working yarn (holding the marker to the WS of your work), and p to the gap that is marked with locking marker. Slip the next st to the right needle without working it. Using the marker to pull, draw up the marked yarn from the WS of your work and place it on the left needle as if a new st (adjusting the side marker, as needed, to work the short row, and then replacing it to its original location). Place the st that you previously slipped back to the left needle and purl it together (p2tog) with the "new" st (closing the gap) and remove locking marker. P1, stop, and turn to the right side.

Short Row 4 (RS): Slip the first st to right needle (purlwise) without working it, place a locking marker on the working yarn (held at the WS of your work), then k to the gap that is marked with a locking marker. Using the marker to pull, draw up the marked yarn from the WS of your work and place it on the left needle as if a new st, then knit it together (k2tog) with the next st on the left needle (closing the gap) and remove locking marker. K1, stop, and turn to the wrong side.

Short Rows 5–8: Rep Short Rows 3 and 4 twice more. Knit to the end of the rnd until you are one stitch before the final gap. Slip this st to your right needle without working it, then, using the marker to pull, draw up the marked yarn from the WS of your work and place it on the left needle as if a new st. Replace the st that you previously slipped back to the left needle and knit it, then knit the next two st together (k2tog) and remove the locking marker. Do not turn.

Your short rows have been completed and your gaps should be closed.

Next Rnd: K to end of rnd.

About the colorwork: You will begin the colorwork chart on the next rnd, working Setup Chart rnds 1–3 once, then repeating Main Chart rnds 1–12 in order as you continue to work the yoke. You will work an increase rnd on every 2nd and 8th rnds as follows. Note that the design is just a 2-st repeat, but the chart shows 6 st to help you envision the pattern more clearly.

SETUP

Work Setup Chart with MC and CC1 over 3 rnds, and then cut MC. (You will not use MC again until indicated.)

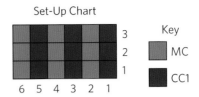

Set-Up Chart

Transition to Main Chart (over 12 rnds), working increases on every repeat of rnds 2 and 8 as follows:

Rnd 1: Work Chart rnd 1 as indicated.

Rnd 2 (inc): K3 (4, 4, 0, 2, 4, 4, 0, 2), [k8, M1R] rep bet brackets to last 3 (4, 4, 0, 2, 4, 4, 0, 2) st, k to end—19 (20, 20, 22, 22, 22, 24, 24) st inc.

Rnds 3–7: Work Chart rnds 3–7 as indicated.

Rnd 8 (inc): K3 (4, 4, 0, 2, 4, 4, 0, 2), [k9, M1R] rep bet brackets to last 3 (4, 4, 0, 2, 4, 4, 0, 2) st, k to end—19 (20, 20, 22, 22, 22, 24, 24) st inc.

Rnds 9–12: Work Chart rnds 9–12 as indicated.

STITCH COUNT CHECK-IN

196 (208, 208, 220, 224, 228, 228, 240, 244)

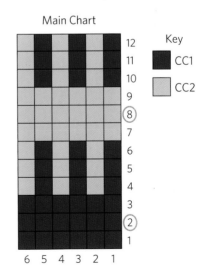

Main Chart

Repeat Two

Rnd 1: Work chart as indicated.

Rnd 2 (inc): K3 (4, 4, 0, 2, 4, 4, 0, 2), [k10, M1R] rep bet brackets to last 3 (4, 4, 0, 2, 4, 4, 0, 2) st, k to end—19 (20, 20, 22, 22, 22, 22, 24, 24) st inc.

Rnds 3–7: Work chart as indicated.

Rnd 8 (inc): K3 (4, 4, 0, 2, 4, 4, 0, 2), [k11, M1R] rep bet brackets to last 3 (4, 4, 0, 2, 4, 4, 0, 2) st, k to end—19 (20, 20, 22, 22, 22, 22, 24, 24) st inc.

Rnds 9–12: Work chart as indicated.

STITCH COUNT CHECK-IN
234 (248, 248, 264, 268, 272, 272, 288, 292)

Repeat Three

Rnd 1: Work chart as indicated.

Rnd 2 (inc): K3 (4, 4, 0, 2, 4, 4, 0, 2), [k12, M1R] rep bet brackets to last 3 (4, 4, 0, 2, 4, 4, 0, 2) st, k to end—19 (20, 20, 22, 22, 22, 22, 24, 24) st inc.

Rnds 3–7: Work chart as indicated.

Rnd 8 (inc): K3 (4, 4, 0, 2, 4, 4, 0, 2), [k13, M1R] rep bet brackets to last 3 (4, 4, 0, 2, 4, 4, 0, 2) st, k to end—19 (20, 20, 22, 22, 22, 22, 24, 24) st inc.

Rnds 9–12: Work chart as indicated.

STITCH COUNT CHECK-IN
272 (288, 288, 308, 312, 316, 316, 336, 340)

Repeat Four

Rnd 1: Work chart as indicated.

Rnd 2 (inc): K3 (4, 4, 0, 2, 4, 4, 0, 2), [k14, M1R] rep bet brackets to last 3 (4, 4, 0, 2, 4, 4, 0, 2) st, k to end—19 (20, 20, 22, 22, 22, 22, 24, 24) st inc.

Rnds 3–7: Work chart as indicated.

Rnd 8 (inc): K3 (4, 4, 0, 2, 4, 4, 0, 2), [k15, M1R] rep bet brackets to last 3 (4, 4, 0, 2, 4, 4, 0, 2) st, k to end—19 (20, 20, 22, 22, 22, 22, 24, 24) st inc.

Rnds 9–12: Work chart as indicated.

STITCH COUNT CHECK-IN
310 (328, 328, 352, 356, 360, 360, 384, 388)

Repeat Five

Rnd 1: Work chart as indicated.

Rnd 2 (inc): K3 (4, 4, 0, 2, 4, 4, 0, 2), [k16, M1R] rep bet brackets to last 3 (4, 4, 0, 2, 4, 4, 0, 2) st, k to end—19 (20, 20, 22, 22, 22, 22, 24, 24) st inc.

Rnds 3–7: Work chart as indicated.

Rnd 8 (inc): K3 (4, 4, 0, 2, 4, 4, 0, 2), [k17, M1R] rep bet brackets to last 3 (4, 4, 0, 2, 4, 4, 0, 2) st, k to end—19 (20, 20, 22, 22, 22, 22, 24, 24) st inc.

Rnds 9–12: Work chart as indicated. Cut CC2.

STITCH COUNT CHECK-IN
348 (368, 368, 396, 400, 404, 404, 432, 436)

Repeat Six

Rnd 1: Work chart as indicated.

Rnd 2 (inc): K3 (4, 4, 0, 2, 4, 4, 0, 2), [k18, M1R] rep bet brackets to last 3 (4, 4, 0, 2, 4, 4, 0, 2) st, k to end—19 (20, 20, 22, 22, 22, 22, 24, 24) st inc.

Rnds 3–7: Transition to Final Chart and work rnds 3–7 to complete the colorwork section. At the conclusion of the chart, cut CC1 and continue with MC only for the remainder of the body.

STITCH COUNT CHECK-IN
367 (388, 388, 418, 422, 426, 426, 456, 460)

> **Note:** Your gauge is likely to get bigger as you transition to the stockinette stitch portion of the sweater. You may need to go down one needle size for the remaining body to maintain the same gauge as the colorwork portion.

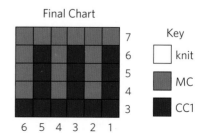

Final Chart

SIZE 1 ONLY

Next Rnd (inc): With MC, k2, [k33, M1R] rep bet brackets to last 2 st, k to end—11 st inc.

SIZES 2, 3, 4, 5, 6, 7, 8, 9 ONLY

Next Rnd (inc): With MC, kx (4, 4, 0, 2, 4, 4, 0, 2), [k19, M1R] rep bet brackets to last x (4, 4, 0, 2, 4, 4, 0, 2) st, k to end—x (20, 20, 22, 22, 22, 22, 24, 24) st inc.

ALL SIZES RESUME

Next 5 Rnds: K to end of rnd.

SIZE 1 ONLY

Move ahead to Divide for Sleeves.

SIZES 2, 3, 4, 5, 6, 7, 8, 9 ONLY

Next Rnd (inc): Kx (6, 0, 4, 6, 0, 0, 2, 4), [kx (18, 17, 16, 16, 16, 16, 17, 17), M1R] rep bet brackets to last x (6, 0, 4, 6, 0, 0, 2, 4) st, k to end—x (22, 24, 27, 27, 28, 28, 28, 28) st inc.

SIZE 2 ONLY

Next Rnd: K to end of rnd, then move ahead to Divide for Sleeves.

SIZES 3, 4, 5, 6, 7, 8, 9 ONLY—CONTINUE

Next 5 Rnds: K to end of rnd.

Next Rnd (inc): Kx (x, 8, 4, 6, 0, 0, 6, 8), [kx (x, 16, 17, 17, 17, 17, 16, 16), M1R] rep bet brackets to last x (x, 8, 4, 6, 0, 0, 6, 8) st, k to end—x (x, 26, 27, 27, 28, 28, 31, 31) st inc.

Next 5 Rnds: K to end of rnd.

Next Rnd (inc): Kx (x, 8, 4, 1, 4, 4, 5, 7), [kx (x, 17, 18, 15, 15, 15, 16, 16), M1R] rep bet brackets to last x (x, 8, 4, 2, 5, 5, 6, 8) st, k to end—x (x, 26, 27, 33, 33, 33, 33, 33) st inc.

SIZE 3 AND 4 ONLY

Next Rnd: K to end of rnd, then move ahead to Divide for Sleeves.

SIZES 5, 6, 7, 8, 9 ONLY—CONTINUE

Next 5 Rnds: K to end of rnd.

Next Rnd (inc): Kx (x, x, x, 1, 2, 2, 1, 3), [kx (x, x, x, 16, 14, 14, 15, 15), M1R] rep bet brackets to last x (x, x, x, 2, 3, 3, 1, 3) st, k to end—x (x, x, x, 33, 38, 38, 38, 38) st inc.

SIZE 5 ONLY

Next Rnd: K to end of rnd, then move ahead to Divide for Sleeves.

SIZES 6, 7, 8, 9 ONLY—CONTINUE

Next 5 Rnds: K to end of rnd.

Next Rnd (inc): Kx (x, x, x, x, 2, 2, 1, 3), [kx (x, x, x, x, 15, 15, 16, 16), M1R] rep bet brackets to last x (x, x, x, x, 3, 3, 1, 3) st, k to end—38 st inc.

SIZE 6 ONLY

Next Rnd: K to end of rnd, them move ahead to Divide for Sleeves.

SIZES 7, 8, 9 ONLY—CONTINUE

Next 5 Rnds: K to end of rnd.

Next Rnd (inc): Kx (x, x, x, x, x, 2, 4, 3), [kx (x, x, x, x, x, 16, 16, 17), M1R] rep bet brackets to last x (x, x, x, x, x, 3, 4, 3) st, k to end—x (x, x, x, x, x, 38, 40, 38) st inc.

SIZES 7 AND 8 ONLY

Next Rnd: K to end of rnd, then move ahead to Divide for Sleeves.

SIZE 9 ONLY

Next 5 Rnds: K to end of rnd.

Next Rnd (inc): K3, [k18, M1R] rep bet brackets to last 3 st, k to end—38 st inc.

Next Rnd: K to end of rnd, then move ahead to Divide for Sleeves.

NEXT SECTION

Before the sleeve divide, you should have the following number of stitches:

STITCH COUNT CHECK-IN

378 (430, 484, 521, 564, 613, 651, 688, 728)

DIVIDE FOR SLEEVES

With MC, k39 (44, 51, 53, 57, 62, 65, 67, 70) st, pm, k111 (127, 140, 155, 168, 183, 196, 210, 224) st—this is the front section. Place next 78 (88, 102, 106, 114, 124, 130, 134, 140) st onto waste yarn—this is the left sleeve. CO 4 st using e-loop (or backward loop) cast-on method, then join to back and k111 (127, 140, 154, 168, 182, 195, 210, 224) st—this is the back. Place the next 78 (88, 102, 106, 114, 124, 130, 134, 140) st onto waste yarn, removing the BOR marker in the process— this is the second sleeve. CO 4 st, placing a new BOR marker in the center of the st, then join to the front.

You have now separated the sleeves from the body and will be working just the lower body as you proceed. You will return to work the sleeves later.

Next rnd: K to end of rnd.

LOWER BODY STITCH COUNT

230 (262, 288, 317, 344, 373, 399, 428, 456)

Continue knitting the lower body in the rnd in stockinette stitch (knitting every rnd) until body measures 12 inches (30.5 cm) from underarm if using superwash yarn (which will grow significantly with blocking). If you're using a natural (non-superwash) fiber and do not expect much growth, continue until the body is 14 inches (35.5 cm) from underarm.

On the next rnd, transition to US 2 (2.75 mm) 24- to 40-inch (61- to 100-cm) circular needle and set up for ribbing as follows:

Rnd 1: K to end, decreasing 2 (2, 0, 1, 0, 1, 3, 0, 0) st evenly using k2tog.

Rnd 2: [K2, p2] rep bet brackets to end of rnd.

Rep rnd 2 until ribbing measures 2 inches (5 cm).

Bind off in pattern with medium/loose tension (not too loose, not too tight). A stretchy bind-off should not be necessary.

SLEEVES

With US 3 (3.25 mm) 12-inch (30-cm) circular needle or DPNs, and beginning with either sleeve, retrieve the sleeve st from waste yarn and pick up the 4 st cast on under the arm—82 (92, 106, 110, 118, 128, 134, 138, 144) st.

When all stitches are on your needle, pm at center of underarm to denote BOR and join to knit in the rnd. Use MC, and work in stockinette stitch (knitting every rnd) for 1.5 inches (4 cm).

Next Rnd (dec): K1, k2tog, k to 3 st before m, k2tog, k1— 2 st dec.

Continue working the sleeve in the rnd in stockinette stitch (knitting every rnd), working a decrease rnd as established every 1.25 (1.25, 1, 1, 0.75, 0.75, 0.75, 0.75, 0.75) inches / 3 (3, 2.5, 2.5, 2, 2, 2, 2, 2) cm until your sleeve measures 17 (17, 17, 18, 18, 18, 18.5, 18.5, 19) inches / 43 (43, 43, 45.5, 45.5, 45.5, 47, 47, 48.5) cm from underarm and you have 58 (68, 76, 80, 78, 88, 94, 98, 104) st (adjust length as necessary for your best fit and to account for yarn growth).

On the next rnd, transition to US 2 (2.75 mm) DPNs and set up for ribbing as follows:

Rnd 1: K to end, decreasing 2 (0, 0, 0, 2, 0, 2, 2, 0) st evenly using k2tog.

Rnd 2: [K2, p2] rep bet brackets to end of rnd.

Rep rnd 2 until cuff measures 2 inches (5 cm).

Bind off in pattern with medium tension (not too tight).

Repeat for second sleeve.

FINISHING

Weave in ends on the WS. Wet block. Soak in lukewarm water with a splash of fiber wash for 20 minutes to gently cleanse and relax the fiber. Press out excess water and lay flat to dry. Turn as needed for even drying.

FINISHED MEASUREMENTS

Neck circumference: 18.25 (18.25, 18.25, 19, 19.5, 20, 20, 20.5, 21) inches / 46 (46, 46, 48.5, 49.5, 51, 51, 52, 53.5) cm

Bust circumference: 33 (37.5, 41, 45.25, 49, 53.25, 57, 61, 65) inches/ 84 (95, 104, 115, 124.5, 135, 145, 155, 165) cm

Length of lower body from underarm: 14–16 inches (35.5–40.5 cm) prior to blocking. Expect at least 2 inches (5 cm) additional growth after blocking, if using superwash or slippery yarn.

Sleeve length: 19 (19, 19, 20, 20, 20, 20.5, 20.5, 21) inches / 48.5 (48.5, 48.5, 51, 51, 51, 52, 52, 53.5) cm from under-arm prior to blocking. Expect at least 1–2 inches (2.5–5 cm) additional growth after blocking, if using superwash or slippery yarn.

Sleeve circumference: 11.75 (13, 15, 15.75, 17, 18.25, 19, 19.75, 20.5) inches / 30 (33, 38, 40, 43, 46, 48.5, 50, 52) cm

Yoke depth (measured on the front, not including back short rows or ribbing): 8.5 (8.75, 10, 10, 10.75, 11.25, 12, 12, 12.75) inches / 21.5 (22, 25.5, 25.5, 27.5, 28.5, 30.5, 30.5, 32.5) cm

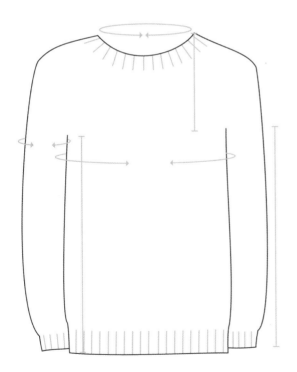

One Skein Beanie

Single skeins in heavier weights can languish for ages without a project, because when it comes to working with limited quantities, heavier weight yarns just don't have the yardage to go the distance. If you're a sweater knitter, like me, you may often buy a little extra "just to be safe" only to end up with a bunch of orphan skeins at the end of your sweater project.

A one-skein hat is the perfect way to put those solo skeins to good use for a quick-knit gift that gives your stash a workout—and the dandelion stitch details work well with nearly any kind of yarn (solid, multicolor, tweed, you name it). No one will ever guess that you were simply "using up" stash yarn for this project!

Skill Level

Intermediate

Construction

Knit bottom-up from the ribbing to the crown (in one piece), this beanie features elongated stitch details that are created by dipping your needle into a stitch on a previous round.

Sizes

1 (2, 3, 4, 5)

Baby (Toddler, Child, Adult Medium, Adult Large)

To fit head size 15.5 (17, 18.5, 21.5, 22.75) inches / 39.5 (43, 47, 54.5, 58) cm

See Finished Measurements on page 117.

Abbreviations

[ ]	brackets indicate a repeat
bet	between
BOR	beginning of row/rnd
DS	Dandelion Stitch: see instructions to right
k	knit
k2tog	knit two st together (dec 1)
p	purl
pm	place marker
rep	repeat
rnd	round
RS	right side
s2kpo	slip 2 st knitwise with working yarn held in back, knit the next st, then pass the two slipped st over the knit st
sm	slip marker
st	stitch/stitches
WS	wrong side

Dandelion Stitch: *Skip over the next st on your left needle and move to the second st. With the tip of the needle positioned at the second st, count down three st, inserting the tip of your working needle into the third st down. Knit into this st and draw the yarn through to your right needle so that it's somewhat loose. Knit 2 st. Insert the tip of your working needle back into the same hole (3 st down) that you previously knit into, and knit into it again, once again drawing the new st out somewhat loosely. Knit the next 2 st. Insert the tip of your working needle back into the same hole one more time (3 st down)—this time it will be a bit more challenging because you'll be reaching backward some distance (you can use a crochet hook, if that makes it easier) and knit into the same hole one more time, drawing up the new st somewhat loosely. Don't count these additional loops as st—you will decrease them away on the next rnd.*

Materials

Yarn	DK or light worsted weight; wool, cotton, bamboo or other fiber blend, 230–250 yards (210–229 m) per 100-g skein, 180 (190, 200, 210, 220) yards / 165 (174, 183, 192, 201) m
Needles	**For ribbing:** US 4 (3.5 mm) 12- to 16-inch (30- to 40-cm) circular needle **For body:** US 5 (3.75 mm) (or size needed to obtain gauge) 12- to 16-inch (30- to 40-cm) circular needle **For crown decreases:** US 5 (3.75 mm) DPNs
Gauge	22 st x 27 rnds = 4 inches (10 cm) with largest needle in dandelion stitch pattern in the rnd, after blocking
Notions	Stitch marker Darning needle to weave in ends Blocking mat **Optional:** Pom-pom

One Skein Beanie Pattern

With US 4 (3.5 mm) 12- to 16-inch (30- to 40-cm) circular needle, cast on 80 (88, 96, 112, 120) st using cable cast-on method. Do not join in the rnd yet. Note that the cable cast-on begins your work immediately on the RS.

Row 1 (RS): [K2, p2] rep bet brackets to end, then pm and join to work in the rnd.

Rnd 2: [K2, p2] rep bet brackets to end of rnd.

Rep rnd 2 until ribbing measures 2.5 (4, 4, 4.5, 4.5) inches / 6 (10, 10, 11.5, 11.5) cm from cast-on edge. The ribbing should be long enough to fold in half. If you are short on yarn (or just in a hurry), work your band half the recommended length for a single width that does not fold.

On the next rnd, transition to US 5 (3.75 mm) 12- to 16-inch (30- to 40-cm) circular needle.

Rnds 1–3: K to end of rnd.

Rnd 4: K3, DS, [k4, DS] rep bet brackets to last st, k1.

Rnd 5: K2, [k2tog, k1] twice, k2tog, [k3, (k2tog, k1) twice, k2tog] rep bet brackets to last st, k1.

Rnds 6–9: K to end of rnd.

Rnd 10: K7, [DS, k4] rep bet brackets to last st. You will use this stitch as the first st in the next dandelion. Skip over this st (the next st on your left needle) and move to the next st (the first st of the next rnd), leaving your marker in place. Continue with DS, slipping BOR marker as you go. You will end 3 st and 2 "petals" of the dandelion past the BOR marker.

Rnd 11: K3, [(k2tog, k1) twice, k2tog, k3] rep bet brackets to last 3 st, one of them being a "petal" from the last DS. K2tog, k1, sm, k2tog, k1, k2tog. K to end of rnd.

Rep rnds 1–11 until body of hat measures 5.25 (6.25, 7.75, 8.5, 9.25) inches / 13 (16, 19.5, 21.5, 23.5) cm from the folded ribbing (fold the ribbing in half and measure from the fold), ending after rnd 6 or rnd 11.

CROWN DECREASES

Note: *Transition to DPNs as needed while you work the decrease rnds.*

Next Rnd (dec): [K5, s2kpo] rep bet brackets to end— 20 (22, 24, 28, 30) st dec.

Next 3 Rnds: K to end of rnd.

Next Rnd (dec): K4, [s2kpo, k3] rep bet brackets to last 2 st, slip the last 2 st together as if to knit, remove the BOR marker, knit the first st of the next rnd, then pass the 2 slipped st over this st. Replace the BOR marker so that the s2kpo stitch is now the last st of the rnd—20 (22, 24, 28, 30) st dec.

Next 3 Rnds: K to end of rnd.

Next Rnd (dec): K2, [s2kpo, k1] rep between brackets to last 2 st, slip the last 2 st together as if to knit, remove the BOR marker, knit the first st of the next rnd, then pass the 2 slipped st over this st. Replace the BOR marker so that the s2kpo stitch is now the last st of the rnd—20 (22, 24, 28, 30) st dec.

Next 3 Rnds: K to end of rnd.

Next Rnd (dec): [S2kpo] rep bet brackets to last 2 (1, 0, 1, 0) st, k to end—8 (8, 8, 10, 10) st remain.

Bind off remaining sts, and cut working yarn, leaving a long tail.

FINISHING

Thread the yarn tail through a darning needle and draw it through just one leg of each bound-off st on the crown.

Weave in ends on the WS. Wet block. Soak in lukewarm water with a splash of fiber wash for 20 minutes to gently cleanse and relax the fiber. Press out excess water and lay flat to dry, taking care not to stretch the ribbing while it's wet. Turn as needed for even drying.

Wear with a folded brim and top with a pom-pom, if desired.

> **Stash Tip:** *Pom-poms are an excellent way to use stash leftovers! Try mixing and matching a few different yarns (colors and weights) in your pom-pom to use up small bits and create a "confetti" pom-pom for your project.*

FINISHED MEASUREMENTS

Head circumference: 14.5 (16, 17.5, 20.5, 21.75) inches / 37 (40.5, 44.5, 52, 55) cm

Top of crown to edge of ribbing (unfolded): 7.25 (8.25, 9.75, 10.5, 11) inches / 18.5 (21, 25, 26.5, 28) cm

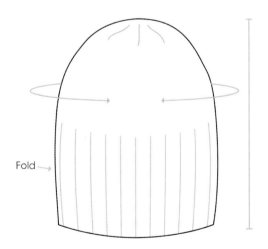

Fold →

Doubling Your Options by Doubling Your Strands

If you're not in the habit of knitting with two strands together, welcome to the party. You're going to love it here! Doubled yarn makes it possible to create a variety of versatile fabrics that can spice up an otherwise simple design. By working with two strands at once, you can create marled, tonal and heathered fabrics, and the results are lovely and interesting.

This technique works best with lightweight yarn, so it pays to keep them in your stash. Fingering weight yarn is my favorite because it's so incredibly versatile, and the higher yardage means more options! When it comes to stash-busting, you can make quick work of twice as much yarn when you knit with doubled strands—even if they're smaller bits and leftovers. In my yarn mixology workshops, I like to give my students a range of lace weight and fingering weight yarns to experiment with, and I am always astounded at the new combinations they create. (For fun, try pairing a hot pink fingering weight yarn with a red lace weight mohair and you'll see what I mean.)

How It Works

One of my favorite things about knitting is that you get to create your fabric while you form the shape of your project, and that fabric can change depending on your yarn and the size of your stitches. Whether you're knitting with single or double strands, your project must still conform to the same principles of gauge that are required for anything you expect to fit on a person. Gauge determines the finished size of a project, and the combination of gauge + fabric will contribute to the look, feel and fit of whatever you're making. Not only do the usual rules of gauge and swatching still apply, but they're twice as important because using two strands increases the number of variables that will affect your results.

Doubling works best with lightweight yarns. If you don't have very many in your stash, may I suggest a shopping trip might be in order so you can see what you're missing? Two strands add up quickly, and if you're not careful, you'll be knitting with super bulky yarn when you meant to make a worsted. This handy guide will help you understand the basic principles of yarn weight and how multiple yarns can work together to create something new and exciting.

One more thing: Working with two strands together can get a little twisty; it's the one downside to this stash-busting method. To counter this, I've found that it's easier to work with two strands when both yarns are wound into center-pull cakes and both are knit directly from the center strands. Because of the nature of knitting, you'll still need to untwist them periodically, but this will keep them from getting out of control too quickly. Whatever you do, do NOT attempt to wind the two strands together into one cake. The strands will not stay together with the same level of tension, and the results will be maddening.

Yarn Weight Guide

Most yarn is assigned a standard weight and is labeled accordingly, but what you might not know is that few yarns—even if they're given the same weight label (like fingering weight or worsted weight)—are exactly the same from one skein to the next. Yarns in the same category can have significant variations in yardage, weight and ultimately, in their resulting gauge. If you're not yet an avid label reader, it's never too soon to start. But the label is only a starting point, and if you're going off the beaten path to create your own double-strand yarns, then you must be willing to commit to a bit of experimentation. It's a necessary ingredient if you want to buck tradition and be the boss of your own yarn.

In addition to the weight and yardage of any given skein, each yarn weight also has a general size rating that ranges from 0 to 5 (lightest to heaviest). These size ratings aren't especially helpful on their own, because they often have very little to do with the gauge you'll actually get from a particular yarn. But size ratings are an excellent place to begin when you're planning to use double strands for a project.

By itself, a lace weight yarn has an official Craft Yarn Council (CYC) size rating of 0, but for the purposes of combining yarn strands, assigning it a 0 value would mean that it has no bearing on the resulting yarn weight when it's held together with another strand. This is obviously not the case, because the addition of a second strand (even if it's lace weight) will affect your results. For this reason, I have assigned lace weight a level 1 identifier, which means it's very light, and I have adjusted both fingering weight and sport weight yarn ratings accordingly. While this may be in slight disagreement with the official yarn weight numbering system, it provides a more accurate method for calculating the results of working with multiple strands.

Here are a few examples of how this method works:

- Two lace weight yarns together (with a size rating of 1 per strand) would equal a fingering weight rating (size 2).

- One lace weight yarn (with a size rating of 1) plus one fingering weight yarn (which has a size rating of 2), will become a size 3 (or DK weight) when they are worked together.

Use the chart below as a starting point to consider how to categorize your potential yarn weights when working with double strands. Please note that this chart is specific to knitting with doubled yarn. Use it as a starting point for blending different weight yarns and for having a rough idea of where to start with an appropriate needle size, but remember that yarn weights vary between brands and different kinds of fiber. So, you will still have to swatch and adjust until you achieve the correct gauge—and have the right overall fabric—for your project. This process is part art, part math, so some creativity is required.

Yarn Weight	Size Rating	Needle Size
Lace	1	US Size 1-2 (2.25-2.75 mm)
Fingering	2	US Size 3-4 (3.25-3.5 mm)
Sport	2.5	US Size 4-5 (3.5-3.75 mm)
DK	3	US Size 5-6 (3.75-4 mm)
Worsted	4	US Size 6-7 (4-4.5 mm)
Aran	5	US Size 7-8 (4.5-5 mm)

When combining yarns, you'll add their size ratings together to determine your new yarn weight. Then refer to the suggested needle size for your new weight as a starting point.

Yarn Weight	Size Rating	Needle Size
Lace + Lace	2	US Size 2-3 (2.75-3.25 mm)
Lace + Fingering	3	US Size 5-6 (3.75-4 mm)
Lace + Sport	3.5	US Size 6 (4 mm)
Lace + Worsted	5	US Size 8-9 (5-5.5 mm)
Fingering + Fingering	4	US Size 6-7 (4-4.5 mm)
Fingering + Sport	4.5	US Size 7 (4.5 mm)
Fingering + DK	5	US Size 8-9 (5-5.5 mm)
Sport + Sport	5	US Size 8-9 (5-5.5 mm)
Sport + DK	5.5	US Size 9-10 (5.5-6 mm)
DK + DK	6	US Size 10-11 (6-8 mm)

You will inevitably come across yarn that defies the rules or doesn't fit into the traditional standards. These numbers are a guide, but they're not the law. If you combine two fingering weight yarns and your fabric looks too loose on a US size 6 or 7 needle, then go down a needle size and swatch until the fabric looks appropriate. These numbers are meant to demystify the process of knitting with multiple strands, but they're just the jumping-off point. In addition to creating the right fabric from your chosen yarn, you need to make sure you also get the proper gauge.

Here's how I approach a new project when I'm planning to knit with double strands:

1. I calculate the new yarn size by adding the ratings for both strands together. For example, if I'm using a lace weight yarn (size 1) and a fingering weight yarn (size 2), I'll be creating a size 3, or DK weight, yarn.

2. If I don't have a particular pattern in mind, I use the recommended needle for the new yarn weight I created (based on the chart on the previous page)—OR if I already have a pattern in mind, I use the needle size the pattern recommends and knit a 5 x 5-inch (13 x 13-cm) swatch. You are probably used to knitting a 4 x 4-inch (10 x 10-cm) swatch, but you'll get far more accurate results for any knitting project if you knit your swatch a little larger so you can measure over 4 inches (10 cm) on the interior of the swatch, away from the edges.

3. I soak my swatch in a small basin of lukewarm water with a splash of whatever wool wash I plan to use for my project. I let it soak for 20 minutes, and then press out the excess water.

4. I pin my swatch flat on blocking mats, pulling the edges taut (but not too aggressively), and let it dry.

5. I unpin the swatch and let it rest for a few minutes before I measure it.

6. I compare the gauge in my swatch to the gauge of the pattern (if applicable) and adjust my needle size, if necessary, so I can match the correct gauge of the pattern.

Gauge can be a bit confusing, so if you've knit a swatch and didn't get gauge, here's how to adjust your needle size:

- If your number of stitches in 4 inches (10 cm) is LARGER than the pattern gauge, go UP a needle size or two and swatch again. For example, if the pattern gauge is 24 stitches in 4 inches (10 cm) and your gauge is 26 stitches in 4 inches (10 cm), go up a needle size.

- If your number of stitches in 4 inches (10 cm) is SMALLER than the pattern gauge, go DOWN a needle size or two and swatch again. For example, if the pattern gauge is 24 stitches in 4 inches (10 cm) and your gauge is 22 stitches in 4 inches (10 cm), go down a needle size.

Once you've achieved the proper gauge and have created a fabric that looks and feels great, it's time to cast on your project!

Marled Stripe Mittens

As we explore the possibilities of knitting with two strands together, I want to introduce the very useful idea of combining varying quantities of yarn of the same weight to create subtle, marled stripes. As with every pattern in this book, these mittens are just the vehicle to illustrate a concept that you can incorporate into any existing pattern that calls for DK weight yarn. You can even knit them with a single strand of DK yarn that achieves gauge, if you prefer. (Though I think it's far more fun and interesting this way, don't you?)

Working with multiple strands in a design like this can help you use up smaller bits of stash that may otherwise be a bit of a nuisance. No one would ever guess that this was a project made of leftovers. These mittens knit up quickly and make a lovely gift for the holidays.

Skill Level

Advanced Beginner

Construction

This pattern is knit with two strands held together: one main color, which is used throughout, and two contrast colors, which are alternated to create subtle stripes. It's knit from the cuff to the top of the hand with a straight cuff (no ribbing) and a Western-style thumb gusset. There is no right or left side for the mittens, as they are each the same and can be turned either way.

Sizes

1 (2, 3, 4, 5)

Toddler (Child, Teen, Adult Small, Adult Large)

Fits wrist circumference: 5 (6, 7, 7.75, 8.5) inches / 12.5 (15, 18, 19.5, 21.5) cm

See Finished Measurements on page 127.

Abbreviations

[ ]	brackets indicate a repeat
bet	between
BOR	beginning of row/rnd
dec	decrease(s)(d)
DPNs	double-pointed needles
inc	increase/increases
k	knit
k2tog	knit two st together (dec 1)
M1L	make one stitch, left leaning (inc 1)
M1R	make one stitch, right leaning (inc 1)
MC	main color
pm	place marker
rep	repeat
rnd	round
sm	slip marker
ssk	slip, slip, k2tog (dec 1)
st	stitch/stitches
WS	wrong side

Materials	
Yarn	Fingering weight, 100% wool or similar, 430 yards (393 m) per 100-g skein | One skein (MC), 90 (100, 110, 120, 130) yards / 82 (91, 101, 110, 119) m
	Lace Weight, silk merino cashmere blend, 224 yards (205 m) per 25-g skein | One skein (Strand 2a) 54 (60, 66, 72, 78) yards / 49 (55, 60, 66, 71) m
	Lace Weight, mohair silk blend, 330 yards (301 m) per 25-g skein | One skein (Strand 2b) 36 (40, 44, 48, 52) yards / 33 (37, 40, 44, 48) m
Yarn Note	**Note:** The MC is held together with either Strand 2a or Strand 2b throughout the project.
	Yarn advice: I've provided general details about the yarn I used to give you a place to start, but I encourage you to test different strands of yarn from your own stash. If you achieve the correct gauge and like the fabric you've created, your mittens will be wonderful.
Needles	US 6 (4 mm) (or size needed to obtain gauge) DPNs
Gauge	22 st x 28 rnds = 4 inches (10 cm) in stockinette stitch (holding two strands together) in the rnd, after blocking
Notions	Stitch marker
	Waste yarn for holding stitches
	Darning needle to weave in ends
	Optional: Crochet hook (size E or F) if using Russian grafting method to close the top of your mittens
	Blocking mat and pins

Hot Tip: *Mittens are meant to be relatively dense, not open and airy. It's possible to achieve gauge but still create a fabric that is too airy for the project. Be sure the fabric of your swatch with both strands is somewhat dense to ensure that the mittens provide warmth to the wearer.*

Marled Stripe Mittens Pattern

With US 6 (4 mm) DPNs and using MC and Strand 2a (held together), cast on 27 (33, 39, 43, 47) st using suspended cast-on method. (See a video tutorial for this technique at oliveknits.com.) Place BOR marker and join to work in the rnd.

Next 4 Rnds: With MC and Strand 2a (held together), k to end of rnd.

Join Strand 2b. Do not cut Strand 2a, but you will not use it for the next few rnds. Carry it along inside your work as you go.

Next 4 Rnds: With MC and Strand 2b (held together), k to end of rnd.

Next 4 Rnds: With MC and Strand 2a (held together), k to end of rnd. Do not cut Strand 2b.

Rep these 8 rnds, alternating Strands 2 as you go until your mitten measures 2.5 (2.5, 3, 4, 4) inches / 6 (6, 7.5, 10, 10) cm.

As you proceed with the following instructions, you will continue in the subtle stripe pattern you've established, alternating Strand 2a and 2b after every set of four rnds. This stripe pattern will continue for the remainder of the mitten.

THUMB GUSSET
Rnd 1: K13 (16, 19, 21, 23), pm, k1, pm, k13 (16, 19, 21, 23).

Rnd 2 (inc): K to marker, sm, M1R, k1, M1L, sm, k to end—2 st inc.

Rnd 3: K to end of rnd.

Rnd 4 (inc): K to marker, sm, M1R, k to marker, M1L, sm, k to end—2 st inc.

Rnd 5: K to end of rnd.

Rep rnds 4 and 5: 3 (4, 5, 6, 7) times more until you have 11 (13, 15, 17, 19) st between your **markers.**

Next Rnd: With both strands, k to marker, remove marker, place next 11 (13, 15, 17, 19) gusset st onto waste yarn, leave the second marker here to mark the side for later decreases and k to end of rnd. The thumb gusset has now been removed from the body of the mitten. You will return to finish the thumb later—26 (32, 38, 42, 46) st.

Working the body of the mitten with the appropriate color combination for your two-strand stripe sequence, knit in the rnd, working stockinette stitch (knitting every rnd) until hand measures 2.5 (3.25, 4.5, 4.5, 5) inches / 6 (8, 11.5, 11.5, 12.5) cm from end of thumb gusset.

Note: *The stripe sequence will end as you proceed to the decrease rnds. For continuity, you may wish to complete your final 4 stripe sequence before you continue, even if it means adding a few more rnds before you proceed.*

Choose either Color 2a or 2b (whichever you have the most of) as your sole second strand for the remainder of the top of the mitten.

DECREASES
Next Rnd (dec): K1, ssk, k to 3 st before side marker, k2tog, k1, sm, k1, ssk, k to 3 st before end of rnd, k2tog, k1—4 st dec.

Rep this rnd until 10 (8, 10, 10, 10) st remain. Cut working yarns, leaving a tail 12 to 15 inches (30 to 38 cm) long for grafting and weaving.

Divide the remaining st in half equally onto two needles so that you have 5 (4, 5, 5, 5) st on front and back. Using either Kitchener st or Russian grafting method to close remaining stitches along the top of the mitten. (See oliveknits.com/grafting for tutorials.) Weave in your ends.

THUMB
Place 11 (13, 15, 17, 19) thumb stitches onto DPNs somewhat evenly and knit in the rnd, working in stockinette stitch (knitting every rnd) and matching the same color and stripe sequence as the corresponding rnds on the body of the mitten until thumb measures 1 (1.25, 1.75, 2, 2.25) inches / 2.5 (3, 4.5, 5, 5.5) cm.

THUMB DECREASES
Next Rnd (dec): [K2tog] rep bet brackets to last st, k1—6 (7, 8, 9, 10) st remain. Bind off remaining stitches.

FINISHING
Cut yarns, leaving a long tail. Thread the tail through the darning needle and use it to pick up just one leg of each bound-off stitch, then draw it through the remaining stitches. Pull tight and weave in ends on the WS.

Repeat these instructions for the second mitten.

BLOCKING
Wet block. Soak your finished mittens in lukewarm water with a splash of fiber wash for 20 minutes to gently cleanse and relax the fiber. Press out excess water. Lay flat on blocking mats and pat into shape, smoothing the edges and thumb—pinning is optional. Turn as needed for even drying.

OPTIONAL
If desired, you can use remaining yarn to create an i-cord string to hold your mittens together (especially for little ones). If you decide to add a cord, make sure it's the length of the arm wingspan from wrist to wrist, plus a little extra for wiggle room.

FINISHED MEASUREMENTS
Circumference around wrist: 5 (6, 7, 7.75, 8.5) inches / 12.5 (15, 18, 19.5, 21.5) cm

Length from cuff to tip: 7.25 (8.5, 10.5, 12, 13) inches / 18.5 (21.5, 26.5, 30.5, 33) cm

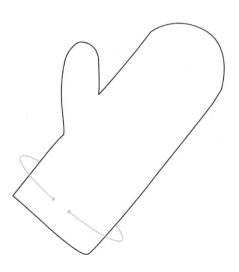

Mini Mohair Cowl

A "mini" is a fingering weight hank of yarn containing about 20 grams and 90-ish yards (82 m) each. Minis do come in other yarn weights, but fingering weight is most common—likely because the heavier the weight, the shorter the yardage (and the shorter the yardage, the more limiting the uses). If you love hand-dyed yarn, chances are you've collected a few minis along the way, and this cowl is the perfect opportunity to use them up.

I encourage you to try matching yarn from a variety of sources. Just because the yarns you've selected aren't from the same company or yarn dyer (or may not even be the exact same fiber content) doesn't mean they won't work well together. In fact, the addition of a strand of lace weight mohair can create a surprisingly cohesive palette when it all comes together.

Skill Level

Advanced Beginner

Construction

This cowl is worked in the round, bottom to top (or top to bottom, depending on how you wear it). It begins with a single strand of yarn until you finish the picot edge, and then transitions to two strands held together and worked in stockinette stitch: one strand of fingering weight + one strand of lace weight mohair to create a subtle buffer between skeins. For best results, I recommend alternating solids and variegated minis, as this provides a more flexible palette and makes the project look intentional rather than haphazard. If you don't have any solid or tonal minis, you can make your own by using leftovers or winding off 20-gram segments from other skeins in your stash.

Sizes

1 (2)

Narrow (Regular)

Circumference: 22 inches (56 cm) for the Narrow version, 24.75 inches (63 cm) for Regular

See Finished Measurements on page 131.

> **Note:** *Height will depend on your row gauge, how many minis you use, and whether you choose the Narrow or Regular option. The best thing about this cowl is that you can easily make it longer or shorter according to when you decide to stop knitting. You can transition to the final edging whenever it reaches the length you like.*

Abbreviations

[ ]	brackets indicate a repeat
bet	between
C1–C7	each color of fingering weight (or similar) yarn will be assigned a number 1–7 to establish the pattern
dec	decrease(s)(d)
inc	increase/increases
k	knit
k2tog	knit two st together (dec 1)
p	purl
pm	place marker
rep	repeat
rnd	round
RS	right side
st	stitch/stitches
WS	wrong side
yo	yarn over (inc 1)

Materials	
Yarn	Fingering weight, superwash merino wool (or blend of similar), 5–7 skeins of 90–95 yards (82–87 m) per 20-g skein
	Lace weight, mohair/silk blend, 1 skein of 500–600 yards (457–549 m) in 50 grams
Needles	US 5 (3.75 mm) 16-inch (40-cm) circular needles
Gauge	24 sts x 30 rnds = 4 inches (10 cm) in stockinette stitch in the rnd, after blocking (stitch gauge isn't super critical, and row gauge will vary)
Notions	Stitch marker
	Darning needle to weave in ends
	Blocking mats and pins

Mini Mohair Cowl Pattern

With US 5 (3.75 mm) 16-inch (40-cm) circular needles and C1 (first mini, until otherwise indicated), cast on 132 (148) st using the cable cast-on method. Do not join in the rnd yet. Note that the cable cast-on begins your work immediately on the RS.

Row 1 (RS): K to end of row, then pm and join to work in the rnd.

Next 2 Rnds: K to end of rnd.

Picot Rnd: [K2tog, yo] rep bet brackets to end of rnd to create the picot folded hem.

Next 3 Rnds: K to end of rnd.

Next Rnd: Fold the hem at the Picot Rnd and turn your work to the WS. Working on the WS, insert the tip of your working needle through the first st on the left needle, as well as the corresponding st on the cast-on rnd. Purl these two st together to begin the fold. Continue this process all the way around, purling the next st on the left needle together with the corresponding st in the cast-on rnd until the entire hem has been folded and secured. Turn back to the RS to continue.

Next Rnd: Join mohair with C1 and hold strands together, working the strands as one as you proceed. Holding both strands, k to end of rnd.

Next 13 Rnds: Holding strands together, k to end of rnd.

Next 2 Rnds: Join C2 with mohair (do not cut C1) and, holding both strands, k to end of rnd.

Next 2 Rnds: Return to C1 with mohair (do not cut C2) and, holding both strands, k to end of rnd.

Next 2 Rnds: Return to C2 with mohair (do not cut C1) and, holding both strands, k to end of rnd.

Next 2 Rnds: Return to C1 with mohair (do not cut C2) and, holding both strands, k to end of rnd.

Cut C1.

Next 24 Rnds: With C2 and mohair, holding both strands, k to end of rnd.

Next 2 Rnds: Join C3 with mohair (do not cut C2) and, holding both strands, k to end of rnd.

Next 2 Rnds: Return to C2 with mohair (do not cut C3) and, holding both strands, k to end of rnd.

Next 2 Rnds: Return to C3 with mohair (do not cut C2) and, holding both strands, k to end of rnd.

Next 2 Rnds: Return to C2 with mohair (do not cut C3) and, holding both strands, k to end of rnd.

Cut C2.

Next 24 Rnds: With C3 and mohair, holding both strands, k to end of rnd.

Next 2 Rnds: Join C4 with mohair (do not cut C3) and, holding both strands, k to end of rnd.

Next 2 Rnds: Return to C3 with mohair (do not cut C4) and, holding both strands, k to end of rnd.

Next 2 Rnds: Return to C4 with mohair (do not cut C3) and, holding both strands, k to end of rnd.

Next 2 Rnds: Return to C3 with mohair (do not cut C4) and, holding both strands, k to end of rnd.

Cut C3.

Next 24 Rnds: With C4 and mohair, holding both strands, k to end of rnd.

Next 2 Rnds: Join C5 with mohair (do not cut C4) and, holding both strands, k to end of rnd.

Next 2 Rnds: Return to C4 with mohair (do not cut C5) and, holding both strands, k to end of rnd.

Next 2 Rnds: Return to C5 with mohair (do not cut C4) and, holding both strands, k to end of rnd.

Next 2 Rnds: Return to C4 with mohair (do not cut C5) and, holding both strands, k to end of rnd.

Cut C4.

Next 24 Rnds: With C5 and mohair, holding both strands, k to end of rnd.

Next 2 Rnds: Join C6 with mohair (do not cut C5) and, holding both strands, k to end of rnd.

Next 2 Rnds: Return to C5 with mohair (do not cut C6) and, holding both strands, k to end of rnd.

Next 2 Rnds: Return to C6 with mohair (do not cut C5) and, holding both strands, k to end of rnd.

Next 2 Rnds: Return to C5 with mohair (do not cut C6) and, holding both strands, k to end of rnd.

Cut C5.

Next 24 Rnds: With C6 and mohair, holding both strands, k to end of rnd.

Next 2 Rnds: Join C7 with mohair (do not cut C6) and, holding both strands, k to end of rnd.

Next 2 Rnds: Return to C6 with mohair (do not cut C7) and, holding both strands, k to end of rnd.

Next 2 Rnds: Return to C7 with mohair (do not cut C6) and, holding both strands, k to end of rnd.

Next 2 Rnds: Return to C6 with mohair (do not cut C7) and, holding both strands, k to end of rnd.

Cut C6.

Next 14 Rnds: With C7 and mohair, holding both strands, k to end of rnd.

Cut mohair and continue with C7 only to the end.

Next 3 Rnds: K to end of rnd.

Next Rnd: [K2tog, yo] rep bet brackets to end of rnd to create the picot folded hem.

Next 3 Rnds: K to end of rnd.

Bind off on next rnd in pattern.

Fold the picot hem in half so that the eyelets create picots along the edge and use a darning needle and the same yarn to tack down the folded edge. Take care to align each st of the bind-off row with the corresponding st on the wrong side, 4 rounds down. Finish tacking the folded edge all the way around, then secure the tacking yarn and weave in your ends on the WS.

Wet block. Soak in lukewarm water with a splash of fiber wash for 20 minutes to gently cleanse and relax the fiber. Press out excess water and lay flat on blocking mats and pin along the top, bottom and sides, taking care to pin the edges flat and even. Turn as needed for even drying.

Hot Tip: *Working with two strands may create color inconsistencies or variations, but these will only add to the artistic beauty of your project.*

FINISHED MEASUREMENTS

Circumference: 22 inches (56 cm) for the Narrow version, 24.75 inches (63 cm) for Regular

Height: 16–24 inches (40–61 cm) from edge to edge

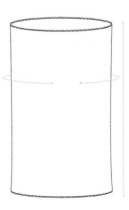

Double Strand Slouchy Cap (Option One)

This classic, gender-neutral cap celebrates the simplicity of stockinette stitch in reverse . . . with a little extra slouch for good measure. Not only does this stylish cap look great on everyone in the family (babies, kids, moms, dads and even teens), but it's also a fabulous project for stash yarn. Even lackluster skeins can be transformed when held together, so search your stash for yarn that might otherwise get missed.

I chose yarn that I had inherited in a stash swap (years ago)—yarn that I was sure would be sitting on my shelf forever if I didn't specifically come up with a way to use it. You may have a few of those in your stash too. Some yarn might seem boring or hopeless on its own, but a project like this can bring those leftovers back to life.

Skill Level
Advanced Beginner

Construction
This cap is knit from the brim to the crown using two strands, held double throughout. It's worked in the round (in one piece) in a pattern called reverse stockinette, which means the purl side (generally known as the wrong side) is facing out. Working with two strands together offers an unlimited number of variations. One of the best things about knitting from your stash is finding a clever way to use skeins that might otherwise gather dust.

Color Pairing Tip
Pairing similar tones of the same color will result in a tonal or hand-painted look. Alternatively, if you choose contrasting colors, your fabric will have a marled appearance. Both are great options! Test the way your strands work together, make sure you're happy with the fabric and don't be afraid to swap something out if it's not giving you the look you want.

Sizes
1 (2, 3, 4, 5)

Baby (Toddler, Child, Adult Small, Adult Large)

See Finished Measurements on page 135.

Abbreviations

[ ]	brackets indicate a repeat
bet	between
dec	decrease(s)(d)
DPNs	double-pointed needles
inc	increase—unless otherwise noted, use the e-loop (or backward loop) increase, as it works best for reverse stockinette
k	knit
k2tog	knit two st together (dec 1)
P	purl
pm	place marker
rep	repeat
rnd	round
RS	right side
st	stitch/stitches
WS	wrong side

Materials	
Yarn	Lace weight, 100% wool or similar fiber content | 2 skeins of 800–840 yards (732–768 m) per 100-g skein
	144 (165, 190, 219, 251) yards / 132 (151, 174, 200, 230) m
	Note: These two strands are held together throughout the project.
Needles	**For ribbing:** US 4 (3.5 mm) 12- to 16-inch (30- to 40-cm) circular needle
	For body: US 5 (3.75 mm) (or size needed to obtain gauge) 12- to 16-inch (30- to 40-cm) circular needle
	For crown decreases: US 5 (3.75 mm) DPNs
Gauge	22 st x 28 rnds = 4 inches (10 cm) with largest needle in stockinette stitch (holding both strands together) in the rnd, after blocking
Notions	Stitch marker
	Darning needle to weave in ends
	Blocking mat
	Optional: Pom-pom

Swatching Tips: *Knit your swatch with both strands held together, then wet block it and pin it flat to dry. For best results, unpin your swatch and let it rest for a few minutes before you measure (always measuring over 4 inches [10 cm]). Don't be afraid to adjust your needle size as needed to achieve the correct gauge. Keep in mind that yarn weight varies between brands and bases—even if they carry the same weight label. Play with a few skeins from your stash to test the double strands together and make sure you're happy with the fabric before you proceed. If it feels incredibly dense or too light and airy, consider swapping something out and swatching again.*

Double Strand Slouchy Cap (Option One) Pattern

With US 4 (3.5 mm) 12- to 16-inch (30- to 40-cm) circular needle and holding both strands together as one, cast on 68 (88, 96, 100, 112) st using cable cast-on method. Do not join in the rnd yet. Note that the cable cast-on begins your work immediately on the RS.

Row 1 (RS): [K2, p2] rep bet brackets to end, then pm and join to work in the rnd.

Rnd 2: [K2, p2] rep bet brackets to end of rnd.

Rep rnd 2 until ribbing measures 2.25 (3, 4, 4, 4) inches / 5.5 (7.5, 10, 10, 10) cm from cast-on edge.

On the next rnd, transition to US 5 (3.75 mm) 12- to 16-inch (30- to 40-cm) circular needle.

Next Rnd (inc): [P34 (44, 24, 10, 14), inc*] rep bet brackets to end of rnd—70 (90, 100, 110, 120) st.

*I recommend the e-loop (or backward loop) increase when working in reverse stockinette.

Next Rnd: P to end of rnd.

Continue working in the rnd in reverse stockinette stitch (purling every rnd) until your hat measures 4.75 (5, 6, 6.5, 7) inches / 12 (12.5, 15, 16.5, 18) cm from the last rnd of ribbing—this measurement should NOT include the rib.

CROWN DECREASES

Transition to DPNs as needed while you work the decrease rnds.

Rnd 1 (dec): [P8, k2tog] rep bet brackets to end of rnd— 7 (9, 10, 11, 12) st dec.

Rnd 2 (dec): [P7, k2tog] rep bet brackets to end of rnd— 7 (9, 10, 11, 12) st dec.

Rnd 3 (dec): [P6, k2tog] rep bet brackets to end of rnd— 7 (9, 10, 11, 12) st dec.

Rnd 4 (dec): [P5, k2tog] rep bet brackets to end of rnd— 7 (9, 10, 11, 12) st dec.

Rnd 5 (dec): [P4, k2tog] rep bet brackets to end of rnd— 7 (9, 10, 11, 12) st dec.

Rnd 6 (dec): [P3, k2tog] rep bet brackets to end of rnd— 7 (9, 10, 11, 12) st dec.

Rnd 7 (dec): [P2, k2tog] rep bet brackets to end of rnd— 7 (9, 10, 11, 12) st dec.

Rnd 8 (dec): [P1, k2tog] rep bet brackets to end of rnd— 7 (9, 10, 11, 12) st dec.

Rnd 9 (dec): [K2tog] rep bet brackets to end of rnd—7 (9, 10, 11, 12) st remain.

Bind off remaining stitches, and cut working yarn, leaving a long tail.

FINISHING

Thread the yarn tail through a darning needle and draw it through just one leg of each bound-off stitch on the crown.

Weave in ends on the WS. Wet block. Soak in lukewarm water with a splash of fiber wash for 20 minutes to gently cleanse and relax the fiber. Press out excess water and lay flat to dry, taking care not to stretch the ribbing while it's wet. Turn as needed for even drying.

Top with a pom-pom, if desired.

FINISHED MEASUREMENTS

Head circumference at brim (stretched): 12.5 (16, 17.5, 18.25, 20.5) inches / 32 (40.5, 44.5, 46, 52) cm

Brim to crown (with ribbing folded in half): 7.25 (7.75, 9.25, 9.75, 10.25) inches / 18.5 (19.75, 23.5, 25, 26) cm

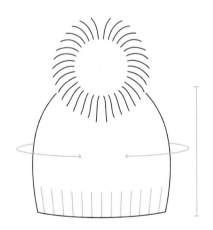

Double Strand Slouchy Cap (Option Two)

This second option increases the versatility of this design by changing up the yarn weight to provide an alternative gauge. It's the same design, and nearly the same fit, but calls for two strands of slightly heavier (fingering weight) wool held double throughout. As with Option One, you can adjust your colors to create a tonal or marled look.

Don't be afraid to try unexpected combinations as you're swatching for your cap. Consider one strand of variegated yarn and a strand of tonal (the tonal yarn can literally "tone down" the look of the busier strand). When in doubt, knit a swatch and see what you think! Some of my favorite combinations are the ones that happened accidentally.

Skill Level
Advanced Beginner

Construction
This cap is knit from the brim to the crown using two strands (both fingering weight), held double throughout. It's worked in reverse stockinette stitch, in the rnd.

Sizes
1 (2, 3, 4, 5)

Baby (Toddler, Child, Adult Small, Adult Large)

See Finished Measurements on page 138.

Abbreviations

[ ]	brackets indicate a repeat
bet	between
dec	decrease
DPNs	double-pointed needles
inc	increase/increases—unless otherwise noted, use the e-loop (or backward loop) increase, as it works best for reverse stockinette
k	knit
k2tog	knit two together (dec 1)
p	purl
pm	place marker
rep	repeat
rnd	round
RS	right side
st	stitch/stitches
WS	wrong side
x	indicates that size is not included in this line of instruction

Materials	
Yarn	Fingering weight, 100% wool or similar, 2 skeins of 420–440 yards (384–402 m) per 100-g skein 144 (165, 190, 219, 251) yards / 132 (151, 174, 200, 230) m **Note:** These two strands are held together throughout the project.
Needles	**For ribbing:** US 5 (3.75 mm) 12- to 16-inch (30- to 40-cm) circular needle **For body:** US 7 (4.5 mm) (or size needed to obtain gauge) 12- to 16-inch (30- to 40-cm) circular needle **For crown decreases:** US 7 (4.5 mm) DPNs
Gauge	18 st x 23 rnds = 4 inches (10 cm) with largest needle in stockinette stitch (holding both strands together) in the rnd, after blocking
Notions	Stitch marker Darning needle to weave ends Blocking mat and pins **Optional:** Pom-pom

Double Strand Slouchy Cap (Option Two) Pattern

With US 5 (3.75 mm) 12- to 16-inch (30- to 40-cm) circular needle and holding both strands together as one, cast on 56 (72, 80, 84, 92) st using cable cast-on method. Do not join in the rnd yet. Note that the cable cast-on begins your work immediately on the RS.

Row 1 (RS): [K2, p2] rep bet brackets to end, then pm and join to work in the rnd.

Rnd 2: [K2, p2] rep bet brackets to end of rnd.

Rep rnd 2 until ribbing measures 2.25 (3, 4, 4, 4) inches / 5.5 (7.5, 10, 10, 10) cm from cast-on edge.

On next rnd, transition to US 7 (4.5 mm) 12- to 16-inch (30- to 40-cm) circular needle.

SIZES 4 AND 5 ONLY
Next Rnd (inc): [Px (x, x, 21, 23), inc*] rep bet brackets to end of rnd—x (x, x, 4, 4) st inc.

*I recommend the e-loop (or backward loop) increase when working in reverse stockinette.

ALL SIZES CONTINUE
Next Rnd: P to end of rnd.

Continue working in the rnd in reverse stockinette stitch (purling every rnd) until your hat measures 4.75, (5, 6, 6.5, 7) inches / 12 (12.5, 15, 16.5, 18) cm from the last rnd of ribbing—this measurement should NOT include the rib.

CROWN DECREASES
Transition to DPNs as needed when you work the decrease rnds.

Rnd 1: [P6, k2tog] rep bet brackets to end of rnd—7 (9, 10, 11, 12) st dec.

Rnd 2: [P5, k2tog] rep bet brackets to end of rnd—7 (9, 10, 11, 12) st dec.

Rnd 3: [P4, k2tog] rep bet brackets to end of rnd—7 (9, 10, 11, 12) st dec.

Rnd 4: [P3, k2tog] rep bet brackets to end of rnd—7 (9, 10, 11, 12) st dec.

Rnd 5: [P2, k2tog] rep bet brackets to end of rnd—7 (9, 10, 11, 12) st dec.

Rnd 6: [P1, k2tog] rep bet brackets to end of rnd—7 (9, 10, 11, 12) st dec.

Rnd 7: [K2tog] rep bet brackets to end of rnd—7 (9, 10, 11, 12) st remain.

Bind off remaining st, and cut working yarn, leaving a long tail.

FINISHING
Thread the yarn tail through a darning needle and draw it through just one leg of each bound-off st on the crown.

Weave in ends on the WS. Wet block. Soak in lukewarm water with a splash of fiber wash for 20 minutes to gently cleanse and relax the fiber. Press out excess water and lay flat to dry, taking care not to stretch the ribbing while it's wet. Turn as needed for even drying.

Top with a pom-pom, if desired.

FINISHED MEASUREMENTS
Head circumference at brim (stretched): 12.5 (16, 17.75, 18.75, 20.5) inches / 32 (40.5, 44.5, 47.5, 52) cm

Brim to crown (with ribbing folded in half): 7.25 (7.75, 9.25, 9.75, 10.25) inches / 18.5 (19.5, 23.5, 25, 26) cm

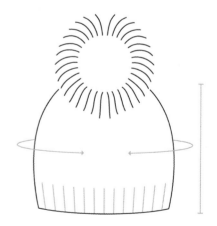

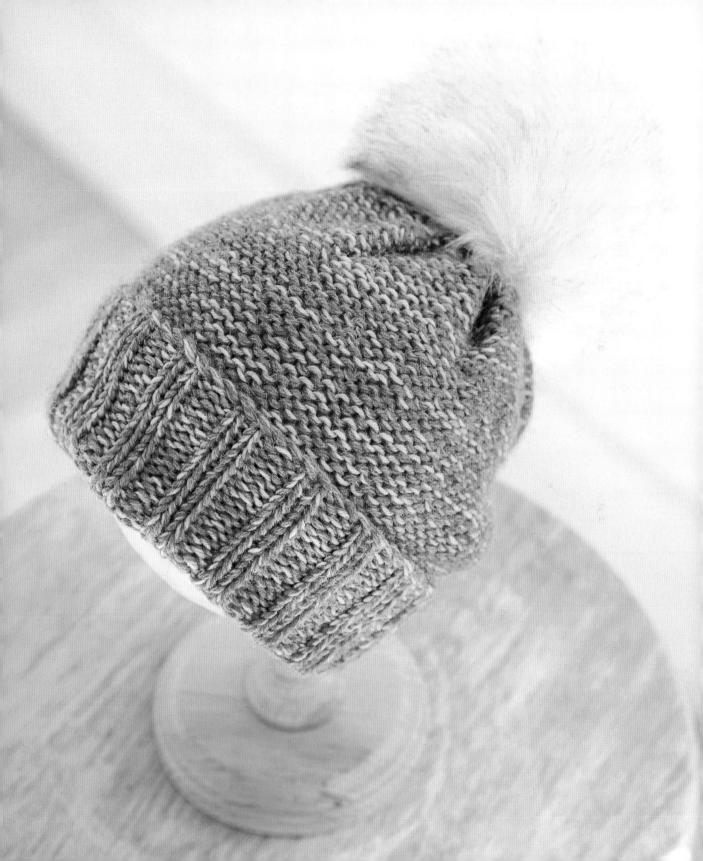

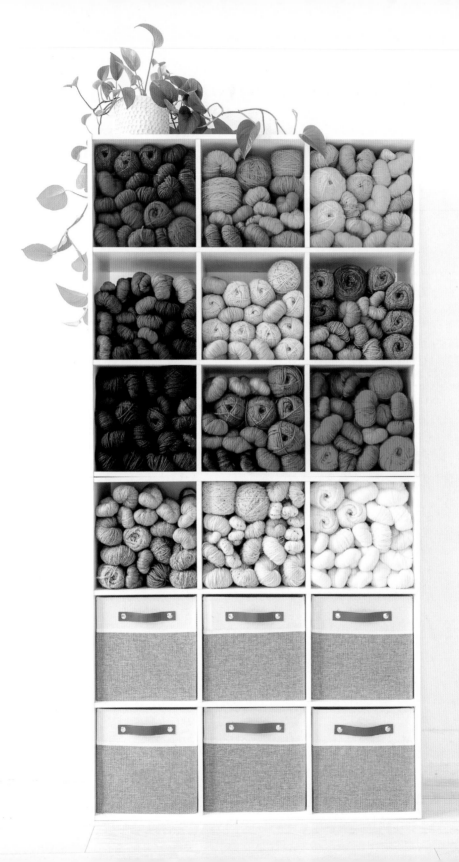

Acknowledgments

I would like to thank the talented and supportive people who helped make this book possible. Many thanks to my tech editor, Bristol Ivy; my sample knitter, Erika Close; my photographer, Annie Loaiza; my illustrator, Carlee Wright; and Rachael Reichmann, for leading the testing, as well as my test knitters: Ashley Grillo, Jeanette Kindle, Kimberly Pellissier, Sharon Peterson, Ellen VanderWey, Erika Field, Kris Odom, Lynette Hansen, Leslie Caponey, Lori Mathieu, Marie Arnett, Sue Nemesh, Kristin Shulman, Nikky Heidel, Joanne Guennewig, Rhonda Kehrberg, Jenn Lewis, Carol Kowalski, Tracy Stratton, Bridget Regan, Becky Clowers, Naomi Schober, Lisa Lewis-Kirk and Gilda Escobar. Thank you to Lisa Encabo for her Cricut skills. Thank you to Page Street Publishing for the opportunity to write another book with them, and my editor, Emily Archbold, who advocated for this book. A big thank-you, as well, to my Stash Sprint students, who shared their stash journeys with me so I could have a wider view of the way knitters buy, store and use their yarn. A big thank-you to every yarn store owner and yarn maker who makes it possible for us to get our hands on beautiful yarn so we have something to stash. Thank you to my Olive Knits team, Carlee Wright and Jessica Shaver, who held down the fort for me when this book kept me busy, and a shout-out to my Knit Camp community for inspiring the work I do. Last but not least, thank you to my family for their love and patience while I locked myself away to write ANOTHER book. And thank you to my bestie, Heidi Hennessy, who cheered me on and provided moral support along the way. You are all my village, and I am grateful for you.

About the Author

Marie Greene is an independent knitwear designer, bestselling author and knitting educator whose innovative approach to seamless knitting has gained notice around the world. Marie is the founder of Olive Knits and Knit Camp, and the author of *Seamless Knit Sweaters in 2 Weeks*, *Knit Shawls & Wraps in 1 Week* and *Knit a Little*. You can find her seamless patterns, renegade knitting tutorials and cheerful tales of her fiber life at www.oliveknits.com. Marie lives in the Pacific Northwest with her husband and two aloof cats. *The Joy of Yarn* is her fourth book.

Index